Spirit
of the
Open Road

The Essential Reference Guide for Canadian RVers

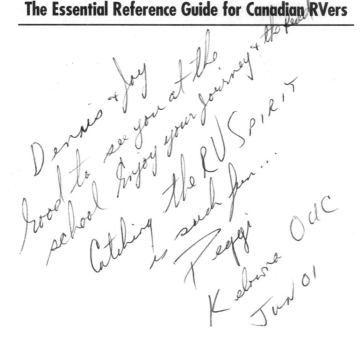

Written by **Peggi McDonald**
Illustrated by **Andrew McTaggart**

WE Publish!

toronto

Printed and bound in Canada.
First edition published 1996 by Wayfarer Explorer Company Limited
1235 Bay Street, Toronto, Ontario M5R 3K4

For John, with love.

When John and I retired, a friend gave us a card with the words, "The future belongs to those who believe in the beauty of their dreams."

This book began as a dream seven years ago - a dream that would never have become a reality without the support and encouragement from family members, RVing friends and others who lent a helping hand.

So many RVers and non-RVers, too numerous to mention, encouraged me and shared their stories and read (and re-read) my drafts. Though both of our families were very supportive, my five sisters, Diane, Nancy, Judy and, my two older sisters, Shirley and Roddy - who though no longer share our daily lives, are still with us in spirit - deserve a special mention. Over the years, one or more has acted as our power of attorney and they've all opened their driveways (and homes) plus made the effort to join us as we explored North America in our RV.

I have to make special mention of my brother-in-law Syd Hills who, very late one night in response to my panicked cry for help, typed my first 15-page seminar hand-out and my sister Diane and her daughter Lianne who, because I was computer illiterate, patiently keyed-in the first two drafts of this book.

So many people have contributed to this book from Dave Young, an RVer friend who first suggested that I put my thoughts in a book to newly-inducted RVers Barb and Joe Martin, who offered encouragement, and Dorothy and Fred Thomsett who, when hearing that John and I needed a place to camp during the final edit of this manuscript, graciously offered us the use of their driveway as a temporary campsite.

This book may have just stayed a dream without the support of Judy Wu and Nikolas Bibassis of the Wayfarer Explorer RV Club. Judy's tireless endeavor and her marketing expertise along with Nick's artistic directions were the crowning touch to our efforts of launching this handguide for Canadian RVers. To my editor at MAS Media Publications and, everyone else involved, thank you all.

However, I dedicate this book to my loving husband John,

who has been there from the beginning. John patiently put up with my early morning writing and accepted the times where we couldn't go "where the road goes" because I had a chapter to complete. I thank him for all the times he accompanied me to a place where he didn't want to be - all in the name of research.

John graciously dealt with the ups and downs of this book and, every time I ran into what seemed an insurmountable roadblock, John never once lost faith. When I faltered, he gently picked me up. Without his expertise in fact-checking, putting up with repetitive on-site editing sessions and his overall suggestions that kept my writing on an even keel, none of this would have ever happened.

Thanks so much for everything, honey. I couldn't have done it without you.

- Peggi McDonald

TABLE OF CONTENTS

Towing

Health & Safety

Fulltiming

The Beginning

"Yes, mother. We bought the RV...
And it's affecting Jack!"

Introduction

My husband John and I bought our first RV in 1985, one year before our retirement from the Canadian military. I was nearing the completion of 26 years in the Air Force and John was ending 33 years in the Navy. In May, 1996, we sold our house and after placing some furniture and keepsakes in storage, sold everything else. Three months later we said goodbye to our military life and jobs and hit the road on the way to our new life.

At that time I was 44 and John was 48. We were also newlyweds (four years) and thought the world was our oyster. Every place we explored was a new adventure and every person we met was a new friend. Our expectations were high and our experience was limited but, somehow, we managed to balance the two even though some of the lessons we learned were not only expensive but also extremely frustrating. Nevertheless, we were free to enjoy ourselves and follow our dreams and 11 years later our journey continues.

Since a posting from one base to another is common in the military, we had excellent training for the nomadic lifestyle of RV travelling. But, unlike being transferred to another base and meeting up with others with a common background, living on the road is a whole new ballgame. Usually the only thing you have in common with your campground neighbour is the fact that your home is on wheels.

Over the years I have had many opportunities to share our experience of the RV lifestyle (or as RVers say, the good life) by talking to others and conducting seminars at RV dealerships and rallies. The first draft of this book was written in those early days. It seemed that everyone we met was hungry for information. The seminars led to our participation as crew members and field reporters for the first 13 weeks of a Canadian RV television series, an experience that went beyond my wildest dreams. This opened the door to writing columns for several Canadian RV publications.

We are still travelling. Our winters are spent in southern hotspots and, in early spring, we head back up to our home base in Ontario and spend the glorious Canadian spring, summer and fall sightseeing and visiting family and friends.

RVing offers a sense of freedom and can be adapted to accommodate any lifestyle. And, it doesn't matter if you're fulltiming or taking your RV out on weekend vacations, all RVers face the same experiences and learn how to cope - usually by trial and error. We were lucky, we had someone to help us through the initial adjustment period.

After we bought our first RV, we spent several months in a campground 20 minutes from work. Our neighbours, Jack and Eunice, were seasoned RVers who explained the ins-and-outs of the RV lifestyle. In my writing I try to be as helpful as these wonderful teaching neighbours.

No matter where we are or what we are doing, we are constantly approached by people eager to take to the open road. Unfortunately, the majority of these people are hesitant and money is the main reason. We have received letters –some polite and some not so polite– saying that they, too, wish they had the money so they could just travel around in an RV.

Well, guess what - neither John nor I are rich, nor are we famous. We live on a pension and manage quite nicely. This book is for all Canadians who are just like us and want to join the good life.

To make your transition to the RV lifestyle as easy as possible, I've grouped related subjects into easy-to-find sections, ending with a handy reference directory. And, because we are Canadian, any costs mentioned in the book are in Canadian dollars.

Buying this book is your first step to this fabulous lifestyle and I know that you're impatient to hit the road. But, wait, before you sell the house and put your furniture and dog in storage, sit back and take a deep breath. You can't join the RV life without -

you guessed it - an RV.

Unless you've inherited a fortune or won the lottery, you just can't walk out the door into a fully-equipped RV custom-made for you. Of course, if you have inherited a fortune, won the lottery or already have your dream-home-on-wheels, skip "The Beginning" and go directly to the next section. ■

To RV or Not to RV

"Frankly sir, his lordship sold
the estate so that he and madame
might become RVers."

You don't need years of experience as a transport truck or bus driver as a prerequisite to get into this wonderful lifestyle. It's actually very simple to learn the basics to jump right in the driver's seat and enjoy your first getaway.

You will make mistakes, however, there are usually friendly RVers close by to help you out of any hot water you land in. Believe me, whenever some procedure such as emptying your tanks or backing into a site seems daunting, someone will be more than happy to offer assistance - whether you want it or not.

And it's surprising how quickly you join the ranks of the "experienced". John and I still laugh over an incident that took place on our first trip when a couple in a rented RV asked John to help them empty their holding tanks. Even though we were so green, we did know more than they did. After all, we had already emptied our tanks for the first time that morning. The great thing about RVing is that as soon as you learn something, it's easy to share the information with others.

Taking each step slow and steady is the key to maximizing your enjoyment of RVing. John and I began our search for our dream home three years before retirement. We knew nothing about RVs but, as we passed a motorhome on the highway one day, we both screamed, "That's what we should do for our retirement!"

Deciding what we wanted to do was easy. Finding a motorhome to do it in was definitely a challenge - we didn't even know a motorhome was called an RV. We were extremely naive and inexperienced about what we wanted, what we needed and where to buy it.

Nowadays, information is fairly easy to come by. We studied the yellow pages for motorhomes and Winnebagos, (we thought all motorhomes were called Winnebagos). At that time we had no idea that the phone book listed the entire scope of mobile travelling homes under recreational vehicles - at least in Ontario. Later on, when we started travelling throughout Canada, we found listings under the categories of travel trailers, vacation homes, mobile homes and trailers. Once we knew where to look, we found dealers with a wide range of inventory located everywhere.

The First Step

What set us on the right road was an outdated magazine that John found at work. Although it was 10 years old, the magazine answered some of our questions but not enough to get us started. I sent away for a subscription. Through the subsequent issues we found dealers, information on various models and a schedule of upcoming RV events in our area.

Until then, we didn't even know there were shows just for recreational vehicles and we quickly decided that this was one event we didn't want to miss. Announcements for upcoming RV shows are advertised on both radio and TV and in newspapers and magazines. In Canada, these annual events are usually held between January and April and are a good place to meet RV dealers, see what the market offers and talk to other RVers.

Neither John nor I will forget our first RV show. We were awestruck by the extensive variety of RVs. There were so many styles, types and models and some were even within our planned budget. We had finally found a place to start us on our way.

We looked at so many models that it was overwhelming. Although shows are an excellent venue for RV shopping, some research before attending helps sort through the maze. Be sure to take notes.

First, look for local RV dealers in the yellow pages and jot down their names. When attending the show, look for their displays and see first-hand what they have to offer.

In some shows the dealers work with the manufacturer so look for a grouping from that manufacturer. Chances are you'll also find representatives from a specific dealership.

Scan local newspapers for dealer promotions - if a big show is being held in your area, the newspaper will probably devote a special section towards the event and dealers will advertise. Also, take a look at the used classified section for private sales. Again, jot down prices so that you will have some comparison price reference when you are at the show.

Most shows have a used RV section featuring pre-owned units from various dealerships. Even though there are good deals to be had when buying privately, first-time buyers should concentrate their search around established dealers. Whether buying a new or pre-owned RV, the dealer's policy of follow-up maintenance plus the availability of experienced personnel to explain the workings of your new acquisition may be worth paying a slightly higher price.

After the show visit as many dealers as possible and familiarize yourself with market availability. If the show was your first, or if you haven't compared prices and makes and models before attending, don't be in a hurry to sign up for your "dream machine" because of a special show price. Most dealers will allow the special show price to stand for at least a week after the show. Talk to the dealer and ask. If you really think that you've found what you want to buy, have one of the representatives write down the make, model, year and type of RV. Record the show price and, this is very important, what features that price includes. Also have the rep note when the price offer expires. Make sure you get the rep's name and call the same person when you are ready to buy. ■

The ABC's of RVing

Recently a non-RVing friend remarked that he and his wife wanted to buy "one of those kind of motorhomes that looks like a bus". He stated he didn't want the type that looks like it's built on a truck. "We want a motorhome," he insisted.

As a matter of fact, both units he described are motorhomes. The bus-style is a Class A and, the one built on a truck, is a Class C. The difference is the design, available storage space and cost.

Don't be fooled by the designation of campers or mobiles or trailers and so on. In actual fact these words all describe recreational vehicles or RVs. If you know the different types of RVs it's easier to determine the style suitable to your lifestyle. Frequently owners of one type can't understand why someone would choose an other. Remember, your RV selection depends on your budget, present and future lifestyle and the time you plan to spend on the road. An RV is not expected to last a lifetime and your first RV will most likely not be your last. As your needs change, switching from one style to another is also possible.

Always keep in mind that there are only two categories of RVs - towable and motorized. Decide what you want and make your choice from there.

Towables include everything from a fold-down tent trailer to the more elaborate fifth wheel. Although the sizes and appointments vary, these models are all pulled by a separate vehicle and require proper hitch devices.

Motorized RVs are self-propelled vehicles. In the motorized category there are three classes - Class A (these look like big buses), Class B (van conversions or those built on a van chassis) and Class C (the living quarters are built right on to a truck chassis with an extension over the cab).

To make the choice easier for you, a brief description of each class follows, starting with the towables.

Towables

❖ Travel Trailers

Travel trailers are what most people think of when they hear the term "mobile home". These towable RVs have been popular since the 1920s. Travel trailers come in many different lengths ranging from eight feet to 40 feet.

In most cases, a travel trailer should not be pulled by a family car so, if you're considering the purchase of a travel trailer, be sure to check the hitch weight required. You'll probably need to upgrade your present car to a heavy-duty model.

Travel trailer styles range from the long, rectangular look to rounded, aerodynamic shapes. Interior designs and appointments vary from model to model but, on the whole, these units are fitted with every amenity found in your home.

"Yeah, it's a 5th wheel all right... you've got to get this plane thing outta your head."

❖ Fifth Wheels

These models are the elite of all the towable RVs. Built with a split-level design, these sumptuous units can make camping in the wilderness seem like a stay in a luxury hotel - without maid service, of course.

Divided into two sections - the kitchen, dining area and living room are on the lower level and, traditionally, the second level (built over the fifth wheel hitch) contains a bedroom and bathroom. Recent models have been introduced with the living room located over the hitch.

The vehicle (truck) needed to pull a fifth wheel can cost the same as the unit itself, raising the total overall price. The tow vehicle must have a heavy-duty V8 or diesel engine and, the longer and heavier the unit, the higher your towing costs.

Because of the size, travel to out-of-the-way spots is limited. This design should not be considered if anyone in your family has difficulty climbing stairs.

❖ Fold-downs or Tent Trailers

Fold-down camping trailers or tent trailers are the popular choice of first time buyers, especially for those with young families who want a weekend and holiday getaway unit. The less costly fold-downs combine all the comforts of home with the thrill of open air tent camping - without having to sleep on the ground.

These collapsible units are constructed on a trailer chassis with the bottom and roof usually made from fibreglass. The collapsible sides can be canvas or a lightweight, waterproof and durable synthetic material. For travelling, the whole unit folds down into itself with the roof acting as a cover.

Easily towed by the family car, set-up takes only a few minutes but, before moving from one site to another, everything has to be packed away in the unit. Fold-downs are suitable for late spring, summer and early fall.

❖ Telescoping or Low Profile Travel Trailers

Low profile or telescoping trailers are a cross between a tent trailer and a travel trailer. Constructed of fibreglass, the unique design of these units allows the top to drop down over the base. When extended, there is usually about 6-1/2 feet to 7 feet of interior headspace.

Low profile trailers offer all the amenities of travel trailers, including full washrooms and ample sleeping space. When the top is lowered for towing, these units offer easy aerodynamic travelling. The low profile roof can also do double duty of transporting a small boat or other equipment without making the unit top heavy. As with fold-downs, there is some set-up time involved.

❖ Truck Campers

Another easy-on-the-budget entry-level RV is a truck camper. Although these units aren't towed behind a vehicle, they do fit on the bed of a pickup truck. Truck campers have evolved from utility units to well-appointed RVs. These units are now available with full three-piece washrooms, stoves and microwaves. With the growing popularity of truck campers, most manufacturers are insulating the units and installing a furnace for year-round use.

Truck campers are available in sizes to fit short and long box pickups and, depending on size, these units can comfortably sleep from two to six people. There's very little (or no) campsite set-up time involved and, when not in use or on an extended stay in a campground, the camper can be removed from the pickup and stored away.

Most towable units include conveniences such as washrooms and kitchen facilities ranging from a full-scale bathroom and complete kitchen to a porta-potti and a two-burner camping stove. However, no matter how elaborate the facilities, when travelling none of these are accessible as they can only be reached from outside of the unit. It is also illegal for passengers to be in the unit when travelling on the road.

Major benefits of having a towable are that these units have a very slow rate of depreciation and command a good re-sale value. There's very little mechanical maintenance required and, whenever your trailer is set up in a campsite, you can unhitch the tow vehicle to use for sightseeing.

Motorized

All other RVs fall under the category of motorized units and, again, the types and styles are numerous. Motorized RVs are simply those that you can drive and are available with either a gas or diesel engine. Styles range from the smaller models to luxurious diesel-powered buses.

One advantage of using a motorized RV is that all facilities are easily accessible. However, moving around must be done with extreme caution and, in areas where seat belt laws are in effect, walking inside your unit when the vehicle is moving is illegal.

Although setting up is extremely easy at a campsite (just connect water and electric), a minor drawback with a motorized RV is the lack of a getaway vehicle for sightseeing and running errands. Many RVers choose to tow a small car behind their unit for this purpose.

Motorized RVs are also the most costly - both in initial cash outlay and replacement. Unlike towables, you don't have the luxury of replacing the tow vehicle one year and the unit the next. Also, because the unit is all-in-one, the depreciation value is greater than that of a towable.

Something to keep in mind if you decide on a motorized RV is that, again unlike towables, when the engine of the motorhome develops mechanical problems, the whole unit must go in for repair. Living in the unit on the parking lot of a garage does not make a memorable vacation.

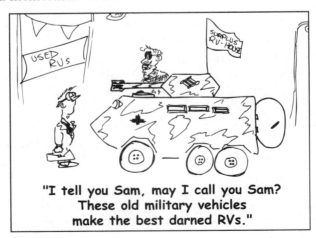

"I tell you Sam, may I call you Sam?
These old military vehicles
make the best darned RVs."

❖ Class A

These motorhomes are the cream of the crop, the top of the

motorhome line and, with the elaborate interiors and varied floor-plans, it's easy to find your dream home. Along with the fifth wheel, these RVs seem to be the main choice for fulltimers.

In recent years, Class As have been built with basement storage compartments. Several years ago, manufacturers raised the inside floor of the units and the space between the floor of the unit and the chassis was transformed into a fairly substantial storage area. Usually accessible from the outside, this area is the perfect place to pack items that "you can't live without".

Some of these spacious compartments contain slide-through areas for skis, ladders, hoses and even an inflatable boat and motor. Another advantage to the basement model is that the driver, co-pilot and passengers all travel at the same height level, unlike non-basement models where the driver and co-pilot sit higher than travelling passengers. Drivers of these high-level basement units must be cautious of wind gusts, tunnel heights and overhead clearance at gas stations and bridges.

❖ Class B

Another member of the motorized group of RVs is the Class B motorhome. Class Bs (or camper vans, van conversions, etc.) look quite a bit like the family van but are taller. With the raised roof and sunken floor, these units have about six-and-a-half feet of interior headspace.

The interiors are more spacious than they appear from the outside. These units are equipped with a comfortable galley, living area and sleeping/dining area. Most Class Bs also feature a toilet and shower, ranging from a full bathroom to a closet that quickly converts into a bathroom with scaled-down amenities. One Canadian manufacturer is now offering a Class B with a spacious slide-out side bath.

The compact size of the Class B offers maximum mobility and can be easily parked almost anywhere. Basic models of this dual purpose vehicle are available for a moderate cost but some, with more elaborate styles, can carry a fairly high price tag.

Although a Class B can double as a family car and sightseeing vehicle, you must break camp before leaving the campground and set up again on return. The limited storage and living space in a Class B may also discourage extensive long-term travel, especially in poor weather conditions. This, however, is not always the case. An RV friend, living in her Class B, proudly described her home-on-wheels this way,

"I have every room in my house but I only have one room at a time. I simply must decide which room I wish to use at the moment."

Incidentally, my friend and her husband travelled extensively in their Class B for many years - their journeys taking them to interesting out-of-the-way places in Europe, Mexico, the U.S. and Canada.

Several companies specialize in van conversions. However, unless the finished product is high enough to stand in, a converted van may be too uncomfortable for prolonged travel. (See Class C for an important fact regarding overloading.)

❖ Class C

Last, but not least, in the motorized group is the Class C. These motorhomes are a smaller version Class A built onto a truck chassis, complete with an overhead cab. The main sleeping area is usually in the cab-over bunk, although there are models with bedroom configurations.

Class C models and floor plans vary from the extremely basic to a more elaborate and comfortable home-on-wheels. Some smaller units are low in height with compact designs. Lengths range from about 14 to 27 feet. These units can do double duty as both a vacation home and a touring vehicle, however, they are often too large and too long to efficiently manoeuvre in many sightseeing spots. Also, if using this class as a tour vehicle, you have to break camp (up awnings, disconnect water, electric and sewer before moving) and set-up again when you return to your campsite. Class Cs, depending on size, are functional for short vacation jaunts and fulltime living.

Since the Class C and Class B have smaller a engine and chassis than a Class A, overloading takes on a stronger importance. Many are already close to their recommended GVWR (Gross

Vehicle Weight Rating) set by the chassis and engine manufacturer. And, this is before luggage, passengers, fuel and water are loaded on.

Storage space is limited and it's quite easy to overload these compact RVs. Carrying too much weight reduces the handling ability plus adds stress to the chassis springs, tires and vehicle components. While this is true for any type of RV, it is more critical in both the Class C and Class B.

For Your Information

❖ Park Models

A park model trailer is in a class of its own and is perfect for those who are looking for a permanent set-up in a trailer park. People who buy park models rent land space at designated "seasonal" campgrounds and use this type of RV in lieu of a cottage.

Usually the unit is placed on a concrete pad and many owners add rooms and porches to extend their living space. You will also see many of these units in a landscaped setting with fences around the lots and driveways with covered parking areas.

❖ Slide-outs

Quite a few RV models offer room extenders or, as they are more commonly called, slide-outs. These slide-outs are available in varying lengths and quite often are considered optional equipment on many towables and motorized units.

Even though these extensions add tremendously to the living, dining and bedroom space, they add weight to the unit. If it's not possible to extend them in narrow campsites, the interior living space may become limited.

With so many different classes, types and models to choose from, the hardest part of joining the RV life is deciding which RV is right for you. Determine what you want your RV for - occasional camping or fulltime living quarters. Make a list of comforts that you simply cannot do without before shopping for your dream home-on-wheels.

If you are planning to live fulltime in your unit (or at least 50 percent of the time) - travel trailers, fifth wheels, Class A or C motorhomes and bus conversions are more comfortable. Take it from an experienced RVer, anything less could turn your dream into a nightmare.

"Yeah...that's Judy's wardrobe trailer, it's in our marriage contract that she gets to take it everywhere we go!"

❖ Rental Units

If you have done your research, attended the shows and are still not sure what type of RV will suit your lifestyle, consider taking a vacation in a rental unit similar to the one you think you might like to buy.

With a rental unit it's easy to experience RV living before putting out purchase money. Renting not only introduces you to the advantages of the RV life, it is also a wonderful way to add variety to your family vacation.

Frequently, vacations in a rental unit are less expensive than staying in a hotel or motel. Campgrounds are cheaper than motels and you can cook and eat your meals in the unit, saving on the expense of restaurants. You can also use the entertainment facilities at most campgrounds and save your money for extra sightseeing jaunts.

In some areas, RV rentals are listed in the telephone book with

RV dealers and, in others, under automotive rentals. If finding a local rental office is a problem, call a dealership. Quite a few dealers keep rental units on hand and, if not, they can tell you where to find an RV rental office.

Start Small

If you're nearing retirement, buy a smaller version of your chosen home-on-wheels. Use it to become familiar with the pros and cons of RV living and, if you decide that RVing is the life for you, trade your smaller unit in for a larger one.

Unlike cars, RVs depreciate at a slower rate (especially the towables) and you can get an excellent trade-in price to put towards a larger unit.

"But Honey, the salesman promised this is an one-of-a-kind conversion... plus he threw in 10 acres in the Everglades for FREE!"

Before You Sign

Whether attending an RV show or a dealer open house, you'll always find an RV that will dazzle you. Look beyond the glitz and glitter, you want the construction to last longer than the "like new" shine.

Most RVs in the same model line and class are fairly equal in looks and features and carry about the same price tag.

Floorplans and colour schemes do differ, but, if you see two similar models with an outrageous price difference, stop and ask why the one is so much lower.

There's a good chance that the one selling at a rock bottom price is exactly that - rock bottom. Construction costs and materials might have been skimped on and, if the price is that much lower, you'll probably end up paying for a host of "options". Paying for options is fine, if the item is really an option.

"We want fuzzy dice, bear skin rugs, gold fixtures, a ping-pong table, bowling alley, swimming pool... are we missing anything thing else?"

Look beyond price and appearance, do not assume that what you see in the unit you are looking at is what you will get. When you contract to buy, have every single thing written on the bill of sale. If a condition of your purchase is the inclusion of an air conditioner or a pair of roof vents or a complete maintenance check at six months or whatever you and your sales rep decide on - make sure that the salesperson writes it down and initials the additions. Unless you have the proof on paper, you might find yourself, once again, digging into your wallet and starting to actively resent your new RV. ■

You've found your dream machine, the price and all the features are right and everything seems to be a go. Hold on a minute - before signing ask yourself if you can live in the RV of your choice.

Have your sales rep leave you (and your spouse) alone for a half hour with the unit. Go inside the RV, shut the door and sit down on the chesterfield and close your eyes. At the count of 10, open your eyes and take a good, slow look around. Take out your checklist and mentally ask these questions, making notes of the answers.

Can you live with the layout of the floorplan? If you answered yes, get up and walk around. Open every drawer and every cupboard to see if the space is easily accessible. Make sure that nothing interferes with the ease of opening.

Check out the location of the bathroom and open the door. Nothing in the way? Great. Now picture the dinette folded down into a bed. Can you still get to the bathroom without climbing over sleeping bodies with the bed down? Or just as bad, will the bathroom door even open if the bed is down? If you are absolutely sure that it will only be yourself and your partner in the RV at all times, then maybe you could live with that "little" inconvenience.

Go right inside the bathroom. Shut the door and sit on the toilet (with the lid down). Is there enough room to move without smacking your funny bone? Can you reach the toilet paper without being a trained contortionist? No problem? Okay, now stand up and pretend you are taking a shower. Is the towel rack located in an area where it will stay dry? Is the bathroom big enough to dry yourself and get dressed without hopping from one leg to another? Look for a vent in the bathroom or at least a window that can be opened. Without either of these, the bathroom will stay damp and you will eventually have a problem with mould.

If the bathroom passed the test, go into the bedroom. Lie down on the bed - yes, both of you - to see if it is wide enough and long enough for sleeping comfort (good way to check the firmness of the mattress, too). Make sure that any cupboards hanging on the wall over the bed aren't so low that you'll bang your head every time you sit up and that at least three sides of the bed have walk-around space. Crawling around a bed to tuck in sheets can become awfully wearing after a while.

Once the bedroom has been okayed, go back to the galley, or kitchen. Stand at the sink and check the height and width of the counter. If the counter is too low, you could develop a persistent backache. If it's too high, you will be straining to reach the faucets. The countertop should be wide enough for a dish-draining rack with a bit of room to spare. Anything smaller will eventually make meal preparation a real chore.

"You're sure we're going to be safe enough for New York?"

The sink should be wide enough and deep enough to hold the required amount of water for the supper dishes. If you plan on living in your RV for longer than one week at a time, a double stainless-steel sink is more functional to wash and rinse the dishes. Most RVs come with a fitted sink cover (to match the counter) that creates additional counter space - a necessity in an RV.

Make sure the stove and fridge doors can be easily opened without banging into a wall and that the fridge door opens wide enough to remove the shelves and crisper drawers. If your RV includes an oven, stand in front of it and fully open the door. Hauling out the roast pan while bending over the side of the door is not very comfortable. Another thing, make sure there is a range hood and fan to remove cooking steam and odours.

Most dinettes are bench-style and the seats do not pull out or push in so, try it out for sitting comfort. If your dinette does fold into a bed, ask your sales rep to show you how to do it and practise a few times when he or she is present.

Examine all cupboards, closets and additional storage space. Check that all doors and drawers have proper latches to prevent them from opening when the RV is in motion. Look for suitable electrical connections and space for a microwave, air conditioner, furnace or TV.

> If your "dream unit" is equipped with a generator, is it large enough to accommodate the style of RVing you have in mind? For short stops at rustic, no-hookup campgrounds, a small "jenny" is sufficient. But, if you like to dry camp (boondocking) for long periods of time, you may need a large auxiliary power unit. Just remember, for every hour a generator operates, it uses three to four litres of gas. Considering gas costs, will you really save money dry camping?

Finally, go back to the chesterfield or easy chair and relax. Pretend you are reading or watching TV. Is there enough lighting for comfort? Can you watch television without lying down or craning your neck?

When you finish your interior inspection, walk around the outside of the RV. Examine all outside storage to locate all valves and holding tanks as well as electrical and hose connections. Having an abundance of storage space adds comfort to RV living. If you plan on winter camping, make sure the unit has proper insulation as well as a standard furnace.

If you choose a motorized RV, take a good look at the engine. Since most of us know only the basics when it comes to engines, I would recommend that you have an independent mechanic take a look at your prospective buy. A qualified mechanic can tell you if the existing engine has enough power to climb a hill in hot weather and if all systems are functioning.

Have your mechanic test drive the unit to ensure that it is in top condition at the time of purchase. If your purchase is new from a dealer, ask (and get in writing) what mechanical follow-up is standard. If you are considering a pre-owned unit, obtain the past maintenance records and let your mechanic go over them.

Investing in an RV is not an impulse purchase so, take your time and do your research. Buying an RV is just the same as buying a house or car - you have to be able to live with your decision.

> *Solar panels and inverters will help to offset power costs when camping without hookups. However, these items may be costly aftermarket accessories. Do your homework, solar panels may or may not enhance your RV lifestyle.*

Ask other RVers what they like about their unit, make a list of what you want and, by all means, shop around. Your satisfaction is the key to enjoying the good life.

Above all, do not become discouraged - eventually, everything will fall into place. After our three year search for our dream RV, we were only 90 percent satisfied with our first purchase. In the 11 years we've been on the road, many things changed for the better.

Finally, we're confident that, although we're not experts, we are able to handle most of what's going on. As the saying goes, "We've come a long way babe!" ■

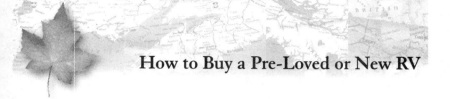

How to Buy a Pre-Loved or New RV

The decision to buy a new or a pre-loved unit has many variables. Again, for each purchase you must do your homework. Our Pace was two years old when we bought her after a three year search and knew what we wanted. She was in pretty good shape with just a few flaws - she'd travelled considerable miles and her former owner had added on electrical toys. Many of his modifications, although important to him, were useless to us and, consequently, never used. Most were in the same condition when we sold the coach as when we bought it.

Another RVing friend purchased an almost-new Class A last year. Although heavily modified with extra propane tanks and every bell-and-whistle, he purchased the fully-loaded motorhome at a fair price. However, he spent a considerable amount of money changing the modifications made by the former owners plus, for safety's sake, he removed one propane tank he felt was too low to the road.

Buyers of pre-loved RVs must be aware that there's almost always some after-sale modification required. On the other hand, you may save thousands of dollars because of the depreciation rate deducted from the original cost of used units.

When purchasing used, kicking a few tires helps. Check under the unit for faulty exhaust and other problems as well. Explore every crevice before you buy. It's possible that some previous modification may be hanging too close to the ground or not working properly. Another point to consider is the availability of parts for an older RV.

If you have friends knowledgeable about RVs, ask for their advice as well. After you read every piece of literature you can get your hands on, pay an expert to give the RV a conscientious once-over. Remember, most sellers only share good things about your prospective RV. Even honest salesmen may miss some nasty buried problems. A fair price may not be the lowest but it is an amount that both the seller and buyer are happy with. When buying from a dealer, the follow-up service could justify paying a slightly higher price than through a private sale.

First time buyers may benefit slightly from buying an almost-new pre-loved coach because dealers and manufacturers rectify or repair most bugs or problems during the first year of use. Since the overall purchase price is lower, you're able to enjoy the RVing life while discovering what's important to you in a home-on-wheels.

If you're planning on buying a used model, be sure to educate yourself. Shop around at various dealers, scan newspaper advertisements and camping magazines to determine a fair selling price for the unit you have in mind. Know what you want before you begin shopping, don't depend solely on the words of sales personnel.

Remember, if a controversy surfaces at a later date, the only words of importance are those in writing. With a private sale, when you drive away, performance responsibility is all yours. On the other hand, when buying from a dealer, a one to three month follow-up service warranty is standard.

When you buy a new unit it comes with the latest accessories and, sometimes, the dealer will even exchange one accessory for another within the price of the coach.

For instance, our new side aisle motorhome came equipped with two 13,500 BTU air conditioners. John and I asked the dealer to remove the bedroom air conditioner and install two Fan-Tastic vents, complete with rain sensors. We wanted one vent in the kitchen and the other in the bedroom. These climate-control accessories are much more efficient for the floorplan of our coach than the rear air conditioner could ever be.

Everyone has their dislikes and I, personally, will never use a gas oven. Simple enough, the dealership staff removed the complete stove and replaced it with a four-burner stove top. Beneath the burners they built a large cupboard to store my pots and pans.

Because the discussion of these changes occurred prior to closure and were agreed on, we didn't have any problems and all accessories and modifications were included in the overall price. Since everything was recorded on our invoice, when we cross borders, there aren't any questions as to what is original and what was an add-on purchase from south of the border. During any inspection, custom officers know exactly what we have and what we may owe taxes on.

> When buying new, always order extra options from the dealer at the time of purchase. Dealers usually acquire many luxuries and accessories in bulk and resell to customers for competitive costs (plus applicable taxes) which become part of the overall cost of your RV. If you add these products "aftermarket", the price will be higher (dealer's retail plus GST and PST). Purchasing these aftermarket items in the U.S. could well exceed your annual duty-free declaration amount. Don't forget to add the Canadian/U.S. exchange rate to the product price.

The year following our purchase either the manufacturer or the dealer repaired any problems (we only had a few). This even included repainting the bottom portion of our coach because the original paint was less than perfect.

One big disadvantage to buying new is that, the day you drive your RV out of the dealership, your coach will depreciate several thousands of dollars. Once again, addressing the question of, "should I buy used or new?" is a dilemma with no one correct answer. Either is a good choice but, only after checking all details and examining each option. If the purchase seems right for you, go for it.

No matter if you decide on new or pre-loved, before deciding on the unit you'd like, make a personal wish list from previous suggestions. Depending on your planned use, storage areas may or may not be a big part of your decision. The capability of your tow vehicle to pull the trailer of your choice is another major factor to consider. If you plan on buying a motorized RV, you will have to decide whether or not you want to tow a car and if your present car is light enough to tow behind the motorhome. If it isn't then you may have to buy another car. That large fifth wheel may be a beauty but make sure that it's practical for your plans - this may not be the type of RV you need if you want to spend your time at a special secluded spot at the lake.

Although some compromise may be necessary, don't purchase an RV because it's a bargain. If it doesn't suit your needs or the floorplan and decor is not to your liking, you won't enjoy your getaways. Remember, no single RV fits every wish list. Set yourself a purchase budget and stick to it, however, buy the most RV you can for your money. Unlike purchasing a house, it's not possible to add a room.

Service Follow-Up

Whether your RV is new or pre-loved, to ensure you receive hassle-free follow-up maintenance use the following as a guide.

1.   Make an appointment by phone and explain each item you want looked at.

2.   Follow up with a fax or letter - problems stated in writing are more accurate than verbal.

3.   As a rule, don't ask for extras the day your unit is in for servicing. Service personnel work by appointment and there won't be any time to schedule items not already allotted on work orders.

Remember that during the spring and summer seasons dealers are extremely busy. If you stay with your coach during repairs, the service is usually faster. The staff tries to complete the work of visible customers first - just to get you on your way. ■

Buying Canadian

Most Canadians are aware that the free trade agreement between Canada and the U.S. opened the door to importing many vehicles into Canada. Ideally, the price should be equal but, when John and I considered all options, we decided to purchase our new RV and our towed car in Canada. One question that we have to constantly address is, "With such a wide southern choice, why not buy in the U.S?"

It all comes down to costs, costs, costs. Although in 1993 it became legal to import a new vehicle from the U.S., the 4.9 percent duty added dollars to any sale. (Under the Free Trade agreement duties will decrease every year until 1998.)

While searching for our 1993 dream machine, we discovered list prices of new, quality motorhomes in the U.S. were less than a bargain for anything other than a clearance model. Trade-in values for used RVs were also extremely low.

Another problem was that vehicles owned by Canadians must be registered in Canada and all gauges on imported vehicles must primarily read in kilometres with miles as a secondary reading. Canadian law requires that headlights glow when the ignition is turned on. Upgrading some RVs made for the American market to comply with our laws can be costly - especially when you have to pay in American dollars. Each U.S. dollar spent costs Canadians approximately another 40 cents.

One very important reason why we didn't choose an American unit is the Canadian Standards seal of approval. Towable or motorized vehicles not manufactured for the Canadian market do not display a CSA Z240 seal of approval to prove that the manufacturer is in compliance with Canadian laws for all plumbing, electrical, gas and propane fittings.

Several makes of American RVs (usually those with RVIA approval seals) come close or already conform to the above regulations and are sold as such, with the price modification built-in. Others are easily modified but, some models cannot meet compliance laws at any price. Before you finalize any RV purchases south of the border, call 1-800-333-0558 (Registrar of Imported Vehicles) to ascertain that the vehicle you're considering is actually welcome in Canada.

RV shoppers will find deals in any country. At first look, prices appear extremely inviting in the U.S. However, check carefully before you buy. Extra costs such as import duties, applicable taxes, U.S./Canadian exchange rates and the costs to modify the RV before it's acceptable for import rapidly increase the overall price.

Even if you save a few dollars, buying in the U.S. is not problem-free. After purchase, it helps to be conveniently accessible to your RV dealer during the new vehicle break-in phase. This may not be possible if your U.S. dealership is a fair distance from your Canadian home base.

> *All duties and taxes are added to the purchase price of imported vehicles after the cost is converted into Canadian dollars.*

Unless you have cash on hand to pay for your RV purchase, if buying in the U.S., another major hurdle you may have to overcome is financing your RV. It is highly doubtful that you will be able to get a loan from a Canadian bank (or other lending institution) for an RV purchased south of the border. American banks and other financial institutions in the U.S. rarely grant loans for non-residents, especially when the collateral can be driven away.

All of the above also applies to other vehicles (cars) and accessories you may want to purchase to enhance your RV life. For the same reasons we decided not to buy our motorhome in the U.S., we elected to stay in Canada for our tow-behind car purchase. Our "Go 4" (our Honda's nickname) was laid to rest and we needed another car. We wanted a late model vehicle but not a new one. Honda was once again our choice because it was one model we could tow "four-wheels down" without having to use a dolly. (See the Towing section of this book.)

A local dealer near our summer stopping spot found us a sporty, white '90 Honda Civic Si at a more than fair price. I added colour coordinated striping from the manufacturer to match the car to our motorhome - a very impressive combination.

Finding a tow bar was our last chore. Our choice for a Towmatic II Stowable-type was not an easy find. Hitch dealers don't stock this item in Canada and it usually takes seven to 12 days for delivery. We found the tow bar we wanted in an RV discount store in Detroit but it would have taken several weeks for an installation appointment.

A local Canadian dealer did agree to attach the tow bar if we drove across the border to pick it up. The hassle wasn't worth it so we decided to order one from a hitch centre in London and wait for it to arrive. We simply took our maiden voyage in Kastle #2 without the car in tow.

One interesting point - at the time, the tow bar was listed at a U.S. sale price, including installation and Michigan state tax for $710 Canadian dollars plus any applicable Canadian taxes and import duties. To order the tow bar and have it shipped to Canada only cost us $814 Canadian plus GST and PST. This, too, included installation and the minimal difference in cost was no big deal. We ended up with Canadian service and no across the border discussions.

Good deals are available in both countries but buying in Canada has its advantages. For instance, our three local dealers (motorhome, car and hitch), were willing to discuss problems or explain confusing areas. We paid no U.S. exchange rate on our money and our Canadian price tags were competitive to the same big ticket items across the border.

No matter where you buy, carefully consider all options. Check out the Canadian dealerships first - it may surprise you.

We found that since Free Trade, Canadian values are now well within line to converted U.S. prices. Remember, a fair price is one that satisfies both the buyer and seller. Paying a rock bottom amount may save you a little cash but cost you plenty in unsatisfactory service.

One added point, both our coach and our car were made in Canada and we're proud of the quality workmanship. General Coach of Hensall, Ontario manufactured our Citation motorhome and our Honda is a product of the automotive plant located in Alliston. Three years later we know that buying Canadian and in Canada was one of our wisest decisions. To date, we couldn't ask for better initial or follow-up service. ■

RVing
Made Easy

"Don't you just love the rustic,
rough and ready life, dear?"

Extending Your Living Space

You did it! You bought your new RV and visions of exciting adventures crowd your thoughts. Although your unit might be big enough for your plans, now that you've brought it home, it looks so small compared to your house that it's difficult to imagine how you'll ever find enough space for all your "must have" comforts.

Don't worry, there are endless ways to conveniently carry special extras in easily accessible places. This chapter explains how to pack plus travel tips, outdoor hints, cleaning ideas, towing and driving techniques and simple maintenance tips to make your travelling life fun and easy.

The first step to actually getting on the road to enjoy your new life is packing your RV. One cardinal rule for RVers is to never overload the unit. That, however, doesn't mean you can't make space for necessities and, keeping these three simple guidelines in mind will help you to adjust.

1. Make your RV a comfortable home so you won't miss your

other home;

2. Utilize every nook and cranny that you can find to extend space;

3. Don't pack things so deep you must dig for them.

Buried items are rarely used. Eliminating non-necessities saves space for important "can't live without" extras and also prevents overstuffed RV cupboards from an occasional explosion.

During the past 11 years I discovered that many items serve more than one purpose. Here is my list of "double duty detail", you can make your own up as you go along.

❖ Add a removable clothes bar on brackets to the shower so it can double as a closet. For wet clothes that can't be dried in a machine, place tension-spring bars across a doorway or hallway as a makeshift clothes dryer.

❖ Tuck folded blankets, jackets and sleeping bags neatly inside of pillow cases. The items are not only out of the way and easily accessible, the "throw" pillows add a decorative touch to your furniture.

❖ Tinted windows contribute to privacy as well as reducing heat caused by the sun's glare. (Note: most window repair companies sell and install aftermarket window tinting.)

❖ Cafe-style curtains on RV windows add warmth to the decor as well as enhancing daytime privacy.

❖ To avoid scratching refrigerator shelves, I dress every glass and metal container in my fridge with non-skid booties. These booties are a circle of plastic mesh held in place with an elastic band. I discovered they also do double duty - nothing moves when I forget to arrange the fridge for travel.

❖ Bread and baked goods stay fresh longer when placed in a plastic tub (to catch crumbs) and stored inside your air-tight microwave or oven.

❖ Electric frying pans double as excellent baking or roasting ovens. These are also convenient to use outside (or inside, if you prefer) for cooking food with an odour, such as fish.

❖ A metric conversion calculator is a must for Canadians travelling south of the border. These calculators are inexpensive and can be used either as a conversion tool or as a regular calculator. (Note: these are easier to find in Canada than they are in the U.S.)

❖ Pringle potato chips travel without turning into crumbs and the container is easy to store in minimal space. The containers also make excellent mailing tubes.

❖ Dawn dish soap (or any other mild dish soap) can be used as a substitute for a gentle shampoo. It also breaks up oil and dirt on John's ball caps and shirt collars so they wash cleaner.

❖ Shampoo (or dish soap) poured on a sponge and spread over the pebbly floor of the shower effortlessly releases dirt. A quick rinse with the shower cleans the floor.

❖ The empty squirt bottles from dish soaps become easy-to-use spill-free containers for adding distilled water to batteries.

> *Though John and I print calling cards on our computer, other RVers pass out self-stick address labels to RVers they meet along the way. The labels conveniently stick into the receiver's address book.*

Everything In Its Place

❖ My all-time favourite tip is a way to create extra drawer space. Attach an ordinary pocket-style shoe rack to the inside of a cupboard door. To add stability, put elastic strips side-to-side across the pockets and fasten with screws to the door. These portable drawers work well in the kitchen to store long or large utensils; in the bedroom for underwear; in the bathroom for shampoo bottles and in a storage compartment for easy-to-find screw drivers and other tools.

❖ When non-slip vinyl mesh, designed for use on boats, is placed beneath kitchen appliances they won't move when the unit is in motion. If you line cupboards with this miracle fabric, dishes or pots and pans also stay exactly where you put them. However, this mesh does destroy the finish of some items such as the bottom of acrylic glasses. Rubber stove and sink mats work much the same way but cutting to size is more difficult.

❖ Hide a key outside your coach for emergency entry. If you misplace your keys as much as I do, it's more convenient to use a spare key than it is to break in.

❖ If your RV has an overhead bunk that isn't needed as a bed, remove the mattress. The resulting space is great to store shoes, dress clothes, bedding and more. If you pack any weight in this bed, adding support straps will keep it in place while driving.

❖ The freezer in our refrigerator is one big compartment. To help organize this area, I purchased a simple one-level plastic-coated shelf. Now everything stacks easier and remains within easy reach.

❖ Eliminating magazine clutter and storing the atlas is always a challenge. If you don't have a corner for book racks, keep them out of sight under the dinette or couch cushions.

❖ An RV with a slide-out extends living space but the available working area for sewing or crafts may still be limited. Try this easy modification - cut a portion from two back legs of a folding table to rest on the couch. The amount removed should allow the top to be level when the two front legs stand on the floor. Now you have a work table that doesn't tie up the dinette.

> *Pop can rings make excellent picture hangers.*

❖ Trying to restrain throw rugs from "walking" can be very frustrating. One way that works is to attach a strip of heavy-duty Velcro (needle side) to the underside of the throw rug. Fasten the opposing piece to your RV carpet. New products such as non-slip mesh and washable polyester felt also help to keep the rugs in place.

❖ Baby wipes work great for quick clean-ups and the plastic containers are the perfect size to store recipe cards, elastics, small tools, etc. List contents on the outside with a magic marker.

❖ Glass liquor bottles travel safe and secure when stored in the bottom half of cardboard milk cartons. Wedge plastic containers between cartons and everything is ready for your next happy hour.

❖ Empty sectioned liquor and wine boxes keep shoes or craft supplies together and in place. I use these sectioned boxes to add a sense of order to my basement storage compartments.

❖ Cafe-curtain rods attached to the base of the bed or just above the floor level of walls creates a perfect place to store shoes.

❖ The new ultra-detergent boxes are convenient containers for audio tapes and toys or a good catch-all for a variety of small items. You can disguise the outside of the boxes by applying self-stick plastic such as MacTac.

❖ Adding adjustable shelves to your RV's short and narrow shirt closets considerably increases the storage capacity. To eliminate creases and minimize the amount of space needed, lay your clothes flat before rolling. To ensure an outfit is easy to find, stack the rolled clothes with the ends visible. One RVer we know folds her clothes and places a sheet of cardboard between each item. She also does this with bedding and towels. Another friend uses empty beer boxes to hold towels and face cloths neatly in place.

❖ With the wide variety of plastic containers and tubs on the market, there's certain to be one available for each task. For instance, items such as socks or underwear stay put when stowed in plastic tubs on a closet shelf. Laundry baskets are great organizers to use under the bed. We keep our long cutting knives on a kitchen shelf in a long narrow cutlery tray. When driving, having cutlery trays in the medicine cabinet keep small prescription bottles securely in place. The advantage of using these products is that everything stays put during a rough ride.

❖ One friend wedges two-inch strips of plexiglass in front of her medicine cabinet shelves. For tall bottles, she places a spring-loaded bar across the shelf. Other RVers attach strips of elastic across these shelves to avoid an avalanche when they open the door at destination.

❖ Jewellery is very difficult to store, however, neck chains and earrings hang neatly on hooks or on a piece of plastic craft mesh attached behind a closet door. One friend uses a round, flat splatter screen to store her earrings. The handle already has a hole for hanging and all earrings are easily seen. I use the partitioned compartments of a fishing tackle box to separate my jewellery pieces.

❖ I always found it a challenge to remember where we had put interesting articles on special places to visit. Now these stories have a home in a folder beside the atlas. Make sure that you regularly eliminate old information because a large collection of pamphlets, maps and magazines all add excess weight.

❖ Car-type litter bags are perfect holders for maps and other travel information.

❖ Large plastic sports bottles filled with your favourite drink are wonderful to have when travelling. However, they don't fit into most RV drink holders. If you add a dual size piece of PVC pipe - one end three inches with four inches on the other end - into the existing holders, your sports bottles will fit. The small end fits the holders and the large end supports the bottles in an upright position.

❖ For objects that need trimming, MacTac or car striping is always a good choice. I made a bathroom shelf from plexiglass and mounted it on brackets. I asked a window repair facility to sell and cut a piece of plexiglass for me. After cutting, they heated the front edge of the shelf and curled it up to create a lip so that items would stay put during vehicle motion. I then trimmed this edge with gold and black car striping, adding a professional touch to my creative modification.

Keeping Your Kitchen Organized

❖ The kitchen in your house or the galley in your RV is probably the most used room in your home. Over the years I've adopted many ideas to help simplify life and lessen the time needed to keep our unit clean and tidy.

❖ Putting washed plastic dishes and containers in the freezer overnight removes most unpleasant food odours and freshens the dishes for future use

❖ Plastic clothes pins make quick and easy re-sealers for bags such as chips or cereal.

❖ To keep potatoes from sprouting, store them with apples. To increase juice in oranges, lemons, limes or grapefruit, either puncture the skin and place in the microwave for one minute or submerge in hot water for 15 minutes. To soften brown sugar, place sugar with apple slices in an air-tight container for several days.

❖ To clean a burned pan add water and cream of tartar, boil for several minutes and wash clean. In an emergency, sand or pine cones also make good pot scrubbers.

❖ Dishes and pots and pans rattle and sometimes break when driving. Eating off of disposable dishes or purchasing an unbreakable supply isn't necessary if you simply place circles of plastic bubbles (available from stationery stores or packing supply stores) between each item. Paper plates or a layer of plastic mesh work equally as well.

❖ I stow glasses in a rectangular basket on a cupboard shelf with plastic items placed in between the ones made from glass - everything stays in place and there's rarely any breakage. John and I use our silver wine goblets which travel very well. Breakable wine glasses also stay put at the back or side of a cupboard when you stretch thin bungee cords across the stems and attach the ends of the cords to eye hooks.

❖ Glasses placed in rubber or styrofoam drink coolers travel well as do colourful acrylic patio glasses. Ribbed portions of worn out socks make super travelling booties for glasses.

❖ Trying to keep pesky bug populations in control, especially ants, is always a problem. You can either buy commercial traps or try some of these home remedies. So far they've worked for me.

❖ Put an Ex-Lax square in a lid with a few drops of water near the entrance points or wrap cloths saturated with bug spray around hoses and cords. Coat all outside hoses and electrical cords with a silicone-based lubricant - bugs hate the oily feeling. Sprinkle ant powder or household cleanser around tires, jacks, hoses and cords. Mice seem to hate the smell of Downy fabric softener sheets, so place these near every entrance point.

❖ Scatter bayleaves throughout cupboards and around openings to deter roaches from making your RV their home. As an added precaution, I remove groceries (even cereal) from cardboard cartons. The cartons may be home to a colony of roach eggs.

❖ RV kitchens are compact and where to put the garbage is always a problem. If placed in a cupboard, it uses precious space. One RVer attached a container to the corner of her counter with small bungee cords and eye hooks.

❖ We prefer to store our garbage out of sight. Copying an idea from our last coach, John cut a hole at the back of a deep cupboard with the opening large enough for a waste basket rim to sink flush with the counter top. Make a wood frame or use fancy MacTac to cover the raw edge of the hole. Adding a colour co-ordinated strip of decorative lace or other material to the top of the container hides the plastic bag and re-sizing a cutting board tops it off. One advantage to this modification is that removing the container allows easy access to items stored at the back of the cupboard. ■

My Favourite Household Tips

"I'm doing the dishes, dear."

Making up a bed converted from an RV couch can be a real stretching experience. I place a fitted sheet over the back of the sofa first before opening the bed flat.

Wall space in an RV is always limited. Those without a viewing place for a photo collage could always arrange their favourite photos behind a cupboard door or on the front of the fridge. Cover the collage or photo with a plastic folder or a piece of plexiglass and your family and special friends are always close at hand.

To stop paper towels or toilet paper from unravelling when travelling, squash or flatten the rolls before putting them on the dispenser. Some RVers prefer to secure their rolls with Velcro strips or bungee cords when breaking camp.

Plastic grocery bags are extremely handy but difficult to store. My newest space-saver is a handmade plastic garbage bag holder - an 18-inch sleeve with elastic at the bottom. Another option is to keep the bags in a shoebox-style plastic container with a lid and stand the container on its end. (These containers can also be used for photos and craft supplies.) An empty paper towel roll is one more space-saving container that will hold up to 10 plastic garbage bags. Electric appliance cords stay neat when stored in empty toilet paper rolls. The rolls can easily be decorated to disguise their original purpose.

Stretch cords (or bungees) restrain numerous items from moving when driving. We probably have two dozen in use in our motorhome and other half-dozen ready for use, especially the 12-inch thin ones. You can make your own bungee by looping an extra large elastic around a piece of dowelling in a half hitch knot.

Taking items off shelves and walls before changing destinations is a pain. However, if you place a small amount of a caulking putty (called strip seal or fingertip caulking - available from hardware stores) on the bottom of objects, nothing moves or falls from display position between destinations. When applied to picture corners or other wall hangings, these won't swing from side-to-side either. This putty holds more securely than sticky products specially designed for this purpose.

To remove sticky residue left on surfaces from tape or putty, etc., simply apply a coating of oil - WD-40 or cooking oil - then work it in and let it set awhile before wiping off. Repeat if necessary. This works on every finished surface I've tried.

However, on fabric or carpet, the oil residue may require a specialized follow-up cleaning. One RV friend swears by a product called "Goo-Gone" available from Wal-Mart and K-Mart stores.

Attaching Velcro with glue holds items in place but it is extremely difficult to remove. Our first motorhome was two years old when we bought it and there was Velcro everywhere. It was ten years old when we sold it and the Velcro was still there.

There are several ways to remove decals from exterior surfaces. Most will soften sufficiently for easy removal with a hair dryer (or a heat gun designed for this purpose). Be careful that it doesn't become too hot. Follow with a coat of denatured alcohol - a good polishing compound and fibreglass wax. WD-

40, along with commercial adhesive removers may also work. If these aren't effective, ask a professional. Other ways may damage your finish which would require refurbishing.

Open containers of Damp Rid (a crystal-type dehumidifier/desiccant sold in humid areas of the U.S.) or kitty litter removes excess humidity in an RV. Simply place these containers of crystals in choice locations and the moisture problem vanishes. Desiccants also come in pouches which work well to control moisture in closets. (I've also found that these pouches eliminate a mouldy smell if you've had a water leak in a hard-to-reach area.)

If your unit is not equipped with a washer/dryer, keeping ahead of the wash while moving from place to place can become a constant aggravation, especially if the park's laundry facilities are limited. For easy hand-washing, try placing a bucket of soapy water in your shower and add your wash before you leave. The agitation created when driving washes the clothes and they are ready to rinse and dry when you reach your destination.

Travelling with your water pump turned off is a wise move. Two RVing friends wished that they had - a bumpy road jiggled their motorhome shower tap open with the pump on. Road noise obscured any sound of running water and, when they arrived at their campsite an attache case of very important papers -- stored in the shower for travelling - was floating.

Unattended water leaks cause numerous problems including wood rot. A drip in one place may be the result of a leak from an opposite corner of your RV. During our early years, one of us left the bathroom tap running for 11 hours - with the sink plug in place. The mess was too extensive to clean with towels and at 11:00 p.m., renting an extractor was out of the question. It was necessary to become creative so, by scrapping the oven broiler pan across the floor, I was able to literally push the water out of the door. Several exhausting hours later, and after a session with the hair dryer plus using the heat from the iron, our floor was, once again, dry.

A few other little adjustments will contribute greatly to your comfort. The couch in our motorhome was not as firm as we liked so we added a half-inch plywood board below the top mattress and then padded the edge for appearance. One RVing friend used oversized elastics to join groups of springs together on her sofa. This helped the springs to work as a unit for greater support.

A small battery-operated fridge fan circulates air and provides effective cooling.

To avoid dented and mangled TV antennas, don't drive away from your campsite with your antenna extended. Using simple reminders helps eliminate this embarrassing and very expensive mistake.

1. Take a large spring-loaded hair clip and place it on your TV antenna handle. When the antenna is up, move the clip to your motorhome's steering wheel, sun visor or a "can't miss" final checkpoint near the doorway of your trailer. If it's there when you're ready to leave - check your antenna.

2. In a motorhome, place a dummy key on a key ring in the ignition when the antenna is extended and hang the dummy key ring on the antenna handle when it's in travelling position.

3. When your antenna is up, hang the RV keys on the antenna handle.

4. Some trailerists tie a scarf to a final check point position.

5. Hang a long "can't miss" decoration to the handle when the antenna is up.

Cats like to scratch so put some carpet around a dinette table leg and introduce kitty to its new scratching post. Suspend a toy on a string and your cat will think the RV is paradise.

To simplify the life of the co-pilot and navigator, purchase an atlas that indicates highway exit numbers. Directions in travel guides and campground directories usually list sites by the closest highway exit number. In provinces or states where exit number coincide with kilometre/mile markers, this type of atlas makes it easy to compute distance. ■

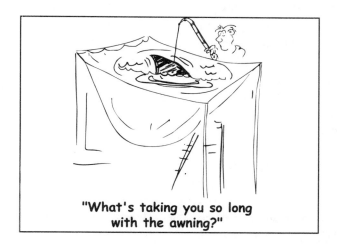

"What's taking you so long
with the awning?"

Just like the RV's interior, there are many little tips you can follow to maintain the exterior and prevent costly repair jobs later on.

Water leaking through the front and back windows is frequently caused by poor caulking around the running lights on the top of the unit. When correcting this problem, remove the lens cover and old caulking of the running lights. Clean the area well then re-seal the running light unit with a bead of silicone. Put the lens cover back on.

For those who aren't mechanically inclined, when removing a battery for winter storage, place a small piece of coloured tape to each wire and terminal combination before disconnecting. Use different coloured tape for each combination and, to re-install, match up the coloured tape pieces.

On sunny days when you would like to keep the main door open but it's too chilly for comfort, winterize your screen door the easy way. Attach a cut-to-fit piece of plexiglass over the screen. With the new "storm" window you can enjoy the sunny day without being cold.

Bike kickstands frequently sink into the soft ground. To keep your bike upright, attach a golf ball to the end of the stand.

One RVing friend carries a rake in his storage area to retrieve those hard-to-reach items buried in tight spaces between compartments. John and I find that the awning stick works equally well (my double duty principle).

Levelling jacks add to the ease of campsite set up. However, be sure the ones you purchase are heavy enough for your unit - our last coach came with an electronic levelling system that would not lift our motorhome. When using any form of levelling system, don't forget to place a pad or board between the jacks and ground or to put chocks behind the wheels to avoid rolling off jacks.

Our neighbour, after arriving late one rainy night in Sault Ste. Marie, Ontario, extended his levellers. The next morning he couldn't move without tow truck assistance as his jacks had sunk deep into the soft ground.

> When you raise your awning, always drop one end several inches lower than the other. Rain water is extremely heavy and needs to drain or the weight will tear your awning or bend the hardware. If you forget to lower one side and water puddles in the middle, take a broom and push the water out before attempting to lower the awning side arm.

Post the CB channel that you monitor on the rear of your unit. We usually tune to #14 and, only occasionally, do we monitor Channel 19. Vehicles travelling behind know how to reach us in an emergency and frequently call to simply say hello. If you're travelling with friends, choose channels other than #13 - Good Sam RVers; #14 - FMCA travellers and, #19 - the trucker's channel.

We often see RVers use green garden hoses to connect their RV to park water supplies. This is a dangerous practice because these hoses are not insulated and the heat generated from the sun creates a perfect atmosphere for bacteria growth. RVers beware – always use the specially designed drinking water hoses to bring water into your RV. It's not only tastier, it's a lot healthier.

Attaching a water hose to the RV city water connection can be a difficult task unless you use a quick disconnect designed for home garden hoses. Place one end permanently on your coach with the opposing end on your water hose and connection is a snap. These handy adapters are also a convenient way to join two hoses together.

In some parks, water pressure surges to an excess of 100 psi. Water regulators, placed at the tap end of the hose, reduce the water pressure to a recommended rate of 45 psi. In one campground, our neighbour's hose split lengthwise creating a beautiful water display. He had his regulator improperly installed at the coach end of the hose. Although it protected his plumbing lines in this position, if the regulator had been placed at the tap end as the manufacturer suggests, the water hose would still be intact.

We know an RVer who was always forgetting his regulator so he attached it to the hose with chain or gun-tape.

Adapters use for filling fresh water tank are sold in RV stores. To make an inexpensive tank filler attach a piece of rubber surgical hose (from the pharmacy) to the male end of a quick disconnect adapter. Connect the adapter to your water hose and place it in the tank.

A good source of fresh water is most important while moving to various destinations. Keeping your fresh water tank pure is easy if purged after storage and at periodic intervals. To purge, add 4-6 ounces of chlorine to 3/4 tank of water and let the water run through your taps until you can smell chlorine. Turn off the taps and, either let the mixture sit in the tank for several hours or take a short drive (to cause agitation), then drain. Refill tank and again drain by letting water run through taps until all of the chlorine odour disappears. Refill tank with fresh water and use as required.

Regular treatment is half a teaspoon to each 10 gallons of water. Remember that every gallon of water or holding tank waste weighs 10 pounds. Choose carefully how much extra weight is actually a necessity. Commercial liquid water purifiers are also available from RV stores but they do cost a little more than household bleach.

"In-line" water filters can be a blessing during your travels. Although park water may test healthy, many campground systems have an objectional taste or smell. Using either a one-unit style or the canister type with removable filters helps to improve quality and odour as well as taste.

Several new RVs include outside showers as standard equipment. If your unit isn't so equipped, make your own outside tap. Place a "Y" connection at the city outlet receptacle on your coach. Add a short piece of hose to one side of the "Y" and, presto, you have an outside tap.

> *If you plan to use your air conditioner, never use an orange or yellow 14-gauge, 15-amp extension cord to connect an RV to electricity. The wiring is not heavy enough to carry the electrical load. A fire may result.*

Seasoned RVers carry at least one extra water hose, a 25-foot heavy duty 10-gauge, 30-amp electric cord as well as a variety of electrical dog-bones and plug-in adapters that connect 15 amps to 30 amps and vice-versa. In many of the new parks we found hookup choices consist of either 15-amp or 50-amp service. These days it's a good idea to include a 50-amp to 30-amp adapter to your collection.

Not all campgrounds are properly wired. Some electric boxes have reversed polarity, others have an open ground and both are dangerous situations if you connect your RV to this source of power. Before connecting your unit to shore power turn the breaker off, test the wiring with a small plug-in tester/monitor then turn the breaker back on. If the monitor reads okay, turn the breaker off, remove monitor and plug in your unit. Turn the breaker on. (Warning - until you check your power, do **not** tie you dog to the RV!

A power line monitor (PLM), temporarily attached to the park outlet or permanently installed in an RV's electrical system, will save appliances from damage caused by electrical surges exceeding 130 volts or when dropping below 102 volts. PLMs simply turn off all power for four minutes or until the problem corrects itself.

When using our generator in a campsite, we now routinely keep the generator door open. Recently, during a large rally, our generator faltered, emitting a loud bang followed by a puff of smoke. We had left our jenny on to run the air conditioner for our dogs, however, we were away from our coach attending seminars. Anxious neighbours couldn't shut it off because we had locked the compartment. Fortunately, no major problem resulted and, both the dogs and the jenny survived.

Dripping water from an air conditioner can make a real mess of the side of an RV. One friend drilled a small hole in the pan below his air conditioner and ran a piece of clear plastic tubing - sealed with silicone - to the ground. A container at the bottom of the tubing is easy to empty and his coach remains clean.

Easy Cleaning

Washing the inside ceilings and exterior of your RV is easy with a long-handled sponge and a no-rinse heavy-duty cleaner. Cleaning the high front of a basement-style motorhome or a fifth wheel can also be a real challenge. This same long-handle sponge with the metal part removed makes the task easier. Apply cleaner with the mop portion and cover with a towel to polish the area to a high shine.

A baking soda and water solution removes tar from vehicles

plus it's a superior general household cleaner. I recently discovered that dipping jewellery into a mixture of baking soda and water makes it sparkle.

If the fibreglass on your RV has a white, chalky appearance, don't waste money on re-painting until you try the easy-to-use cleaners designed to remove oxidization from fibreglass boats. We apply Meguiar's brand of Heavy Duty Oxidation Remover (#44 or #49) with a soft cloth, let it dry to a haze and wipe it off to reveal a lustrous shine. Follow with a coat of one-step RV/boat cleaner and wax (#50). The dullness disappears and your RV will glisten like new. These products are sold in marinas and car/boat supply stores. If you can't find it locally, call 1-800-833-8814 to place an order. Similar products are available for RVs and boats with aluminum exteriors.

If you don't have a dulling problem, use one of the new ultra UV-protection cleaner/wax products sold in RV stores. Find one that needs the minimum effort to apply and wipes off to a shine.

Spray-on tire shining products make your tires look like new. These products also offer UV-protection but look for brands without petroleum in the ingredients since petroleum is damaging to rubber.

Controlling black streaks is always a hassle and the above mentioned products are also good for this. But another favourite is Lysol Tub and Tile Cleaner - the foam type - which not only effortlessly removes persistent black marks, but also leaves a smooth finish, especially on a fibreglass skin.

Another way to protect the skin of your coach, and proudly display decals and stickers from places you've visited, is to attach a cut-to-fit piece of plexiglass to your ladder. Have an autoglass company punch holes into the edge of the plexiglass, thread through heavy-duty ties and you're all set to go. If you sell your coach, remove the plexiglass and your "on-the-road" mementoes stay with you.

My hints could go on and on. As you travel the highways, you'll find other RVers who love to share their special living tips as well and, eventually, your list will triple mine. ■

Parking an RV would be easier if dealers offered lessons to new RVers. Since this doesn't happen very often, newcomers to this lifestyle must learn handling techniques from their mistakes.

Watching inexperienced RVers is a very interesting form of campground entertainment and some perform a most creative and humorous act from the time they pull up to their site until they actually settle in. Although it's hilarious to watch the gestures, it's somewhat embarrassing to hear the frustration of rising voices. And, none of us should laugh because we, too, were all new RVers at one time.

If both the driver and co-pilot practise manoeuvring their unit until they are comfortable - including backing into a site - the rising tempers, knocked over picnic tables and crunched hookups would be a thing of the past.

Some RVers actually fear reaching their destination because

their chosen park may not include pull-through sites and it may be necessary to back into a camping spot. Until both occupants understand a few basic driving hints, routine parking of their unit will always be a challenge plus a source of many spousal arguments. In reality, once you learn, backing a large recreational vehicle into a campsite is actually a simple procedure.

One tip all RVers should follow when backing a motorhome into position is to place your hand at the bottom of the steering wheel and turn the wheel opposite to where you want the rear of your unit to move.

But, when backing a trailer into a spot, place your hand at the bottom of the wheel and turn the wheel the same direction you want the rear of the trailer to move. Remembering the above information helps immensely when backing up or parking an RV.

Several RVing friends prefer to talk each other into a spot. They use a walkie-talkie in conjunction with their CB. No one even becomes excited as the co-pilot guides their unit into place, usually on the first try. These compact transmitters are available from RV stores, Canadian Tire or Radio Shack, etc.

Other RVers are more comfortable backing up with an expensive back-up camera system. Viewing a TV on the dash provides a complete picture of what's behind their coach.

One more group (usually novice) continue to think it helps to stand at the back of the RV and shout commands. I'm sorry, but no driver can hear nor understand voice signals over the noise of an engine. Obviously, some RVers don't understand this point because frantic expletives echo over the campground. There are also a few who feel especially fit and strong because they attempt to stop an RV by pushing or leaning on the back of it as they scream "Stop!"

John and I prefer to use hand signals. We find it easy to back up our motorhome and these same principles apply to trailers or fifth wheels.

Both of us can direct our RV into a tight parking space without frustrating problems. When using such signals, the only major point to remember is the co-pilot must always be in full view of the driver's side mirror (if the co-pilot can see the mirror, the driver can see him or her). RVers have no specific signs to learn, nor is there a right or wrong way to guide someone into a site. As long as both the driver and co-pilot understand what each other is saying with their hands, the signals are effective.

> When using the "buddy system" to park your RV, make sure your co-pilot stands well back of the RV and always remain visible in the side mirror.

At times, fellow RVers want to help, especially the men who feel that women aren't as knowledgeable as males in this area. If someone tries to help John and me, we simply thank them very much and continue using our own signals. No driver can receive direction from two sources. We (both of us share the driving) know exactly how to explain moves to the other with hand signals. Outside help only confuses the issue.

With a little practice, you, too, can settle into your spot with expertise, relax in a lawn chair and wait for the evening entertainment to begin. There will always be several inexperienced RVers attempting to back into a site somewhere.

If you choose to use hand signals, you can develop your own variation. Your main goal is to communicate in simple gestures without yelling or screaming. Happy parking! ∎

Driving Safe

"Dear, I've just installed a co-pilot seat for you."

I can't stress enough that good driving practices improve only after you feel confident handling your vehicle. Whether it's your first car or your first RV, it's wise for both pilot and co-pilot to become comfortable and proficient behind the wheel. Even if one person does most of the driving, a co-pilot never knows when he/she may have to take over in an emergency.

Large shopping centre parking lots - after hours, of course - double as spacious training grounds for parking and backing into places. Until you feel confident, travel on quiet secondary roads to gain experience driving or towing that extra long and high loaded RV.

If you feel some professional instruction may help, contact a truck-driving school and sign-up for their basic course. If it's a bit costly, remember so is your RV. Even a local defensive driving course to update old habits could be a benefit. Taking control of your RV, instead of it controlling you, is the most important consideration. Practise makes perfect in many things but, especially in driving.

It's one thing to be confident on nice, sunny days but, it's impossible to predict what the weather conditions will be after you set out on the road. During one of our seminars, we picked up these tips on driving in adverse weather conditions.

Rain

When it first starts to rain, the roads become slick because of the water mixing with oils on road's surface. This is especially apparent during a light rain or a heavy morning dew. Be careful, because until the road dries or the traffic increases, many roads can become as slippery as a skating rink. When driving in these conditions keep extra stopping distance between you and the vehicle in front. Reduce your speed so that you're not constantly using your brakes (braking too hard and too suddenly can cause you to slide). In heavy rain, when the water builds up on the roads, your vehicle will lose traction and hydroplane (ride on top of water) which makes your brakes virtually ineffective. If you must pull off the road, slow down before you move onto the shoulder. This is extremely important because the gravel shoulders are also very slippery when wet. When stopped, use your four-way emergency flashers to alert other drivers that you have stopped.

Never drive with four-way flashers on in poor visibility conditions. Drivers behind you may think that you've stopped and will pull into a lane of oncoming traffic to move around you.

Fog

Contrary to what you may think, high beam headlights reduce visibility in fog conditions. Because the fog acts like a reflector, the bright lights of the high beams bounce back and impede your vision. Always use low beams when driving in the fog.

If the fog is thick and you can't see, pull off the road to the extreme right shoulder and put on your emergency flashers. Never turn your headlights on or sit in the dark. Vehicles approaching from behind will think that you're either still mobile and on the road or, won't be able to see you at all and, in all probability, will plough right into you.

The safest stopping place is at a gas station or rest area parking lot. Eventually the fog lifts (especially true for morning fog) but, in low lying areas, it remains dense for a longer period of time. Remember, if you can't see anyone else, they can't see you.

High Winds

If your vehicle is being buffeted by high winds, reduce speed and keep both hands on the steering wheel. Hold wheels in a forward direction and don't oversteer to compensate for the swerve caused by semi-trucks passing or when your RV is struck by wind gusts.

Again, practise makes perfect, especially when learning to cope with the increased height and weight of your RV. At first, use secondary roads as much as possible. The lower traffic volume at reduced speed builds confidence and improves handling techniques.

Winter Driving

Even if the weather is mild when you start out, an unpredictable front can change a pleasant drive to one fraught with worry. Any driver living or visiting a snow area should carry an emergency survival kit.

Always have a working flashlight, flares and triangles on board. Flares and triangles are especially important as they illuminate your vehicle during emergency stops and alert other drivers to a potential problem. Flares work well at dawn, dusk or in weather conditions when visibility is low. You can buy flares at RV, automotive and department stores. Although the standard types are lit with a match for one-time use, the new battery operated flares are reusable.

Fluorescent triangles are the second most important accessory carried in your vehicle. These warning devices fold for packing and easily unfold for use. Because of the reflective surface that glows in the dark or shines brightly in the sunlight, triangles are a definite plus to have on board. In an emergency situation, put your flares or triangles about 300 feet in front and behind your vehicle.

> *Keep your windshield-washer tank full and your wipers in good working order - you never know when you'll need them.*

In some parts of North America (in mountainous regions) tire chains are mandatory to travel through passes at high elevations.

Sand or rocksalt (or kitty litter) helps traction. If you get stuck, sprinkle some in front of the drive wheels. Pieces of old carpet may help provide traction. For extra traction, use good all-season radial tires.

Heavy work gloves help when handling icy chains and jacks. Ice scrapers, de-icing fluid and paper towels should be kept on hand to clean windows. In a freak snowstorm, a shovel may be a life-saver if you have to dig out. Always carry 12 to 15 feet of heavy gauge jumper cables.

Last, but not least, if travelling in the winter carry a personal survival kit. Include boots, warm clothes (for layering), plenty of water and emergency high-energy rations. Make sure that you have candles and holders (for heat and light), waterproof matches and paper bags. Paper bags can be placed on your feet, hands and on your head (with eye-holes cut out). Do not use plastic bags. Plastic will suffocate you, while paper allows you to breathe and provides insulation from the cold. Since most of our body heat is lost through the head, keep your head covered. Include a fully-stocked first-aid kit. Make sure you check and replace supplies as needed on a regular basis.

Snow And Ice

The first rule when driving in blowing snow is to never travel with your high beam headlights on. (Read the fog section for the reason.) When driving in cold-weather conditions, you must always expect to run into ice. Because they are so difficult to see, ice patches, especially black ice, are extremely hazardous. Slow down and never slam on your brakes. If your brakes lock in position, you will lose control of your steering and go into an uncontrollable skid. In light snow and on thin ice, heavy vehicles have the stopping advantage, however, when the ice is thick and the snow is packed, your heavy vehicle will slide farther than a smaller car.

In these conditions, reduce speed and increase the distance between you and the vehicle in front. Just like driving a car, be prepared and don't take foolish chances, especially when travelling on snow-wet roads. Remember, most bridges, ramps and overpasses become icy before the road does. Slow down.

When conditions are poor and visibility is drastically reduced, wait until the weather improves. If you're on the road, pull into a rest area and move into your home on wheels, turn the jenny on and relax. No appointment or timetable to be somewhere is worth the risk of an accident and your life.

Mountain Climbing

In a large or heavy RV, always climb mountains in low gear to save wear-and-tear on your transmission. When descending a steep and lengthy slope, especially where it indicates that trucks should use "low gear", gear down. Let your engine do the braking and, never use your brakes to control your speed in this situation.

John and I learned this lesson - also the hard way. Travelling through Oregon our first year, we put new brake pads on the motorhome when we came out of Mexico. On our route north, we climbed a four-mile steep grade before descending for seven miles.

Unfortunately, neither of us was aware of engine braking. Since we had new brakes, we descended using the brakes to control our speed. We were passing a truck at the five mile descent mark when the overpowering smell of burning brakes hit us. Of course, we thought it was the truck. Thankfully, for us, we decided to stop at a rest area around the next bend and discovered that it was our RV with hot brakes. Once again, the good Lord and our guardian angel protected us from a major disaster while teaching us a valuable lesson.

For anyone driving in the mountainous regions of the western states, there is an excellent book, the *Mountain Directory for Truckers, RV, and Motorhome Drivers*, written by Richard Miller, that is a great help to RVers when assessing grades and wondering what's around the next bend. Having the *Mountain Directory* on board takes the guesswork out of mountain driving. For a copy write or call: Mountain Directory, R & R Publishing Inc., P.O. Box 941, Baldwin City, Kansas 66006, phone number (913) 594-4054.

Drive Alert

Most experienced RVers drive short distances every day, with frequent stops. The stops (especially if you do some sightseeing) can make getting there part of your travel adventure. A large percentage of accidents are caused by driver fatigue. The following hints may help you keep alert (and alive) when driving.

Change drivers frequently if your driving day is long. Only sit behind the wheel if you're well-rested.

If nighttime driving is uncomfortable, arrange your schedule so that all driving is done in the day. Since I began wearing glasses all the time, headlights reflect and cause a glare to the point where my vision is less than perfect. Both John and I drive after dark only when it's unavoidable and, even then, for just a very short distance.

Eating helps you to stay awake but adds unnecessary calories. Try chewing gum (like your life depends on it) and you'll accomplish the same effect without adding extra pounds.

Don't take any medication (either prescription or over-the-counter) without carefully reading the label. Some drugs may cause drowsiness and put you to sleep. Be very careful when mixing medications, mixing could cause adverse reactions and decrease driving ability.

A little coffee keeps you awake but, too much coffee can act in reverse and cause you to nod off. And, save the partying for after your arrival - drinking alcohol or suffering from a hangover doesn't mix with sitting behind the steering wheel of a moving vehicle.

"Harold... it's an RV, NOT a ship!"

Recognize the signs of drowsiness, such as yawning and heavy eyelids. Stop the vehicle and change drivers. If this isn't possible, stop the vehicle (in a safe place - a truck stop or restaurant), and take a nap or, at least, take a walk-around break as soon as possible. Frequent stops sometimes help drivers cope with drowsiness.

Keep the inside of your vehicle cool with a breeze on your

face. It's easier to stay alert in cool temperatures and your passengers can always cover up if they get cold. Turn the radio on to an interesting talk show or strike up a conversation with your travel companion. You can also talk to yourself when there's no one else around. Who knows, that may prove to be the most informative conversation of your life and you know that the response will be what you want to hear. Ignore the strange looks from others in passing vehicles, talking will keep you awake and that is your top priority.

Tire Safety

A few weeks before trading in our previous RV, we narrowly escaped a complete wipeout because of poor tires. A lady driving an older model car was passing us on an interstate when a van following too close forced her into our lane. As she began pulling over, her right rear tire blew. It pushed her towards the inside shoulder, directly into the path of the van. No one was badly hurt because both vehicles were moving at the same speed and both drivers retained control of their vehicles. Had the rear left tire blown, she would have collided with us resulting in a much different ending.

Tires are one of the most important parts on your RV and your tow vehicle. Learning all you can about tires may mean the difference between an enjoyable vacation and one overflowing with problems.

If your unit has dual tires, spend the money on a quality set of valve extenders. When checking air pressure, it's extremely difficult to reach the tire valves on the inside tires of a dual system. With a valve extender, one end fits on to the valve and the hose is clamped on to the wheel hub allowing easy access when needed to read or increase tire air pressure.

It's difficult to put air into RV tires at a service station. Having a three-quarter horsepower air compressor on board to inflate your tires while still in the campground simplifies this whole procedure.

Braking Tips

All brakes should be periodically tested, especially after driving through water. In wet weather, to avoid locking your brakes, apply pressure (brake, release, brake, release, etc.) until your vehicle can be safely stopped. With an automatic transmission, you can maintain better control on slippery roads if you shift to neutral or, with a standard tranny, depress the clutch. This disconnects the drive wheel so it won't compete with the brakes. Don't brake and turn at the same time. When turning, momentarily remove your foot from the brake.

Anti-locking brakes are now being built into most vehicles. Anti-locking brakes automatically go through the brake/release, brake/release action as soon as the brake is depressed so, there is no need for the driver to pump the brake. There is a weird feel to the brake pedal and a different kind of noise with anti-lock brakes. Don't panic - keep your foot on the brake.

According to the Ontario Ministry of Transportation and Communications in its driving pamphlet titled *Good Driving Practices*, there are three main types of braking on good road conditions. Contact the Department of Transport for pamphlets containing other hints for drivers.

Threshold braking - this is when you press as hard as possible on the brakes without locking up or skidding the wheels. Release pressure if wheels lock and re-apply - don't pump the brakes.

Steering around an obstacle - is another way to avoid an accident. Use the threshold braking method and then steer to the left or right. If you must enter another lane, check to make sure it's clear.

Four-Wheel Lock braking - is when a quick stop is mandatory. Hit the brake as hard as you can and hold it to lock the brakes. This is the fastest way to stop but, with locked brakes, the car continues in a forward direction and you have no steering capabilities.

Other points mentioned in this pamphlet are rules that I knew at one time but have forgotten over the years. One tip that a whole slew of other drivers have also forgotten is to keep a safe stopping distance from the vehicle in front of you. Some roads have measured chevrons painted on the surface to indicate the safe distance. If there aren't any chevrons, take note of a check-point (hydro pole, etc.) on the side of the road. When the car in front comes to that point, count off "one-thousand and one, one-thousand and two". Drivers following at a safe distance will not have reached the same check-point before the count is finished.

Adjust your driver's seat to a comfortable position. The seat should be close enough so that your left foot sits flat.

Before starting the ignition, adjust all rear-view and side mirrors (clean if necessary) so that the mirrors are positioned for optimum viewing suited to the height of the current driver.

Watch for blind spots and frequently check all mirrors for traffic conditions both behind you and to your sides.

Be extremely cautious of children and animals in suburban neighbourhoods - they have a habit of darting out on to the road without looking.

Watch for open car doors in your path or for other vehicles pulling out without warning. Be wary of bicycles, mopeds and motorcycles. Give road maintenance workers a "brake" as well.

Always signal, you may know where you're going but others don't unless you signal your intention. This is especially true when you are constantly travelling the same route. Signal, don't assume that the other driver is as familiar with the road as you.

Keep a driver's handbook with emergency road rules handy in your glove compartment. Take it out every once in a while to familiarize yourself with emergency guidelines.

If possible, keep a cell phone with you whether you are in your RV or your car. Being able to call for help in any situation offers additional peace of mind.

Driving skills depend on good reflexes, wise judgement and treating other motorists as you would like to be treated. At this time, RVers don't need a special licence to control very heavy vehicles and driving preparation or extra road training is almost non-existent. Give yourself an edge by doing your own extra training - a little practise and preparation is all it takes to increase driving skills and improve your on the road travel. ■

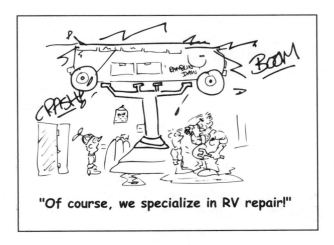

"Of course, we specialize in RV repair!"

Most of the time RVs perform exactly as you expect them to, however, on occasion problems do surface. Of course, this only happens when you are away from home and in unfamiliar territory. When your home-on-wheels or your tow or towed vehicle requires some TLC, the following tips may help you find a quality repair facility.

Ask a local RVer or campground staff where they have repairs done. On one occasion we stopped for gas in the small town of Van Horn, Texas. We were leaking coolant and the attendant sent us down the road to a repair shop. There, helpful mechanics replaced a rad hose clamp and pressure-tested the radiator for a mere $5.00 (1991 prices).

Call your emergency road service (ERS) personnel for a recommendation. Once, when we had minor valve problem on our tag axle compressor on a late Friday afternoon, I phoned various shops for service. After continually hearing, "No, we can't look at it until Monday", I called our ERS. The agent stayed on the line until we found a facility to look at our problem. The shop agreed to repair it - if we didn't need new parts. We were on our way in 15 minutes.

Many vehicle manufacturers provide a toll-free help line. Look for yours in the operating manual. Before you leave Canada, make sure that the toll-free number works from the U.S. Get a regular phone number and ask if they have an international toll-free number.

If your engine needs looking at, take your unit to a Chev, GMC or Ford, (etc.) dealer; your tires to a speciality shop such as Goodyear, Firestone or Michelin. Have an oil change done at a service centre that specializes in quick turn-around service. If your RV needs repairs, call an in-park service company or take it to an RV dealer.

Camping World, a discount RV chain of stores, is located throughout the U.S. and their service is second to none when it comes to RV repairs. All the work carries a warranty plus, if one store does the repair, a second store will honour the service contract if you run into any problems.

When you have found a qualified facility, be considerate. Make an appointment, if possible. Travellers simply dropping by can pose a difficult problem for mechanics who already have a full workload.

Give the service manager a written list of required maintenance or repairs. Include your vehicle identification number (VIN) and your mileage. When your request is in writing everyone understands what maintenance you are requesting and the service manager can schedule sufficient time for proper repair. Ask for an estimate - it may come in handy later if charges differ from what you expected.

In all cases, plan to stay with your vehicle or RV at the facility. The service you receive will be faster and, possibly, of higher quality when you are visible. Staff simply want to complete your work and get you on your way.

If you must leave your vehicle for extended periods (major

engine jobs), pre-arrange a set time every day to discuss problems with your mechanic. An RVing friend of ours blew the engine on his towed car. Because he had important commitments 160-km away, he left his car at the garage for a week with promises of completion on his return. Guess what, when he called a week later, the mechanic had run into problems and the car wasn't ready. Our friend had to modify his travel plans. A daily phone call to the service manager may have eliminated this delay or at least prepared him for altered plans.

Ask to see the parts that the mechanic plans to install and for the return of all parts removed from your unit. Another hard lesson learned - once we left a garage with mismatched spark plugs. When another mechanic discovered the mistake, we informed the dealer who made the error. Thankfully, he refunded our full parts and labour costs.

On a different occasion (same situation) only five of the eight plugs were replaced and at one maintenance tune-up, a plastic fuel filter was used instead of a metal one (needed for larger and hotter engines). One more reason to check all parts before installation.

Our emergency repairs have been quite minimal over the years, mainly because we strongly believe in preventive maintenance. During most years, we stay well under our maintenance budget for both our motorhome and car.

All RVs, towed and tow vehicles need periodic service. Most RVers set up a maintenance schedule to remind themselves of when and how often their vehicles need checking or replacing.

Regular car-style maintenance is required for spark plugs and cables, air filter, battery charge system, distributor cap and rotor, fuel filters, belts and hoses, PVC valve and, if your unit has them, points and condenser.

When you are setting up your maintenance schedule calendar, remember to have your brakes and fuel lines, shocks and suspension system checked. Inspect your tires for wear, etc., and have your coolant system flushed.

Approximately once a year to 18 months have a wheel alignment done and your bearings repacked.

It helps if you purchase a mechanic's helper book. Shop around, you may find one specific for your unit or, collect handouts at mechanical seminars. Sometimes these manuals help mechanics at repair facilities to understand the problem.

Attending a national convention at one of the larger RV clubs is a perfect way to learn more about RV maintenance. At the conventions, experts from various engine and chassis manufacturers hold seminars to teach you how their chassis and engines work. Other seminars cover diesel engines and a host of other mechanical topics. The information gathered here is worth more than the price of the convention.

> *Don't forget to change your oil and filters. This is especially important for diesel engines.*

Some RVers feel more comfortable when they carry easy-to-store spare parts in their RV. Even though many of us can't fix even minor problems, there's usually an RVing neighbour or friend who can do the repair if you have the required part.

Regular RV maintenance should include inspection (and replacement if needed) of non-mechanical items, such as water heaters and furnaces.

Most appliances are extremely reliable accessories, however, all propane appliances should receive an annual preventive check-up by an authorized dealer licensed to perform propane repairs.

> *RV appliances are built for use on vacations or short getaways. If you plan on spending an extended period away or are full-timing, expect to replace appliances, such as your water pump, water heater or, even your toilet at regular intervals.*

Your carpeting and furniture in your RV is used more than they would be in a house. If the furniture requires repairs or modification, attend to it immediately. The dusty environment that RVers live in at many destinations doesn't help and demands extra-special care in cleaning and maintenance.

We have dogs, however, I don't like living with sheets or blankets covering my furniture. In our case, I made decorative seat covers for the couch, captain's chairs plus the pilot and co-pilot seats. The covers take the beating, blend in with our decor and are easy to remove for washing away day-to-day dirt and dog hair.

Excess wear on carpets is the other main concern in an older RV. We've tried correcting this several ways. In our previous coach we removed the carpet and replaced it with a sub-floor of mahogany covered with a heavy-duty vinyl. I simply loved it. For an added touch and warmth, I placed throw rugs throughout the coach. Cleaning with a broom and dustpan was a dream. A quick wash and wax restored the shine. It was amazing to see how much dirt and dust was tracked into the coach every day.

In our present coach, we have carpeting with area rugs placed on top for added protection. These rugs not only protect the carpet, they are easy to take outside for thorough cleaning.

Getting To Know Your Appliances

When we began our extended travels, I could never remember which RV appliances functioned on electric, propane or, occasionally, from the engine battery. These simply exceeded my realm of comprehension.

Mastering the art of living with a 30-amp service carried its own long list of frustrations. I quickly learned that if I operated the fridge on propane every once in a while, I had extra power to use an air conditioner, the microwave, coffee pot and the toaster. If I turned some appliance off, I could even add the TV and my curling iron to the list - without blowing a fuse.

I eventually learned to "trust" these appliances until, one

time, two days after arriving in Mexico, I was overwhelmed by the smell of ammonia. There wasn't a repair facility within miles.

Searching through all available RV maintenance manuals, we discovered everything about the fridge's operation, except how to correct, drain or cope with ammonia leaks. In these manuals we found no repair suggestions, nor did we find out what would happen if we just left it. Apprehensive and unsure of what health related problems may arise, we slept for three nights with the main doors of the coach open. We did find out later that this wasn't necessary. If we had kept the fridge door closed, the aroma of the ammonia coolant solution would have remained trapped inside the well-insulated fridge.

Our refrigerator was an absorption-style model and the only repair person within a 50 kilometre radius was overbooked with work. Even though he couldn't come to our rescue, he assured us that the strong odour was not life-threatening and took time to explain how to remove the plug and drain the ammonia cylinder.

The only long-term remedy for leaking coolant is to replace the fridge and, since we couldn't get another one in Mexico and it wasn't feasible to drive 1,000 kilometres to return to the U.S., we had to deal with our problem for a while (from December to March).

To keep our fridge cold, I put triple-bagged ice in the crispers and placed a large covered cake pan filled with ice in the freezer compartment. They both needed replacing every two days. A refrigerator-freezer is very well-insulated and the temperature remained a constant 40 degrees Fahrenheit, as long as we only opened the door when absolutely necessary.

No make-do solution is ever perfect but, on the other hand, it's better than ruining a perfectly good vacation. At least with having a non-running ice-packed fridge we didn't have to worry about exact levelling the coach at the various campsites we visited.

If your batteries say "maintenance free" check the "eye" for charging instructions. To make sure all other batteries work as expected (and hold a charge) always top up your batteries with distilled water every month, especially if you're in a hot climate.

Fridges and other RV appliances do malfunction and, as a rule, help is usually nearby. RVers whose adventures take them to interesting out-of-the-way places may also take them away from convenient repair shops. A breakdown doesn't necessarily signal an end to your travels but it may tax your imagination to learn how to cope when an appliance doesn't work as expected.

Delays associated with unscheduled maintenance and repairs can be upsetting. Nevertheless, these are only minor irritations RVers must put up with in exchange for the freedom to explore and most RVers feel that working and maintaining a home is much more stressful than a few minor maintenance irritations usually encountered in your home-on-wheels. ■

Understanding Your Sanitation System

Travelling along the highways with bathroom facilities close at hand is one of the many benefits of exploring by RV. But, like all things, this convenience is quickly taken for granted until the toilet does not work. During our first years on the road we made just about every mistake possible and encountering preventable problems with our marine-style toilet was no exception. Hopefully, with a few tips that we've accumulated from personal experience, you'll avoid many of our costly mistakes.

Emptying holding tanks is easy - you simply pull a lever and the contents drain through a hose to the campsite receptacle or into the dump station. Be a considerate camper and always leave a sewer area the way you'd like to find it. If you are a new RVer, get instructions from the dealer on how your system works. If this isn't offered, ask for it.

When draining your tanks, always dump the black (toilet) tank first, followed by the grey (kitchen/shower) water. This leaves your hose fresh and clean and ready for storage and your next hookup.

Remember, all RVers, even those driving the elaborate condos-on-wheels must empty their holding tanks. Some RVers don rubber boots, coveralls and gloves to dump but, if your hose is in good shape and long enough to reach the receptacle, emptying your tanks is really a clean, simple and trouble-free task.

RVers constantly learn lessons from life on the road. My most embarrassing holding tank learning experience was on our first weekend out. We checked into a park without sewer hookups on a Friday night and both of us had showers Saturday morning. John and I knew nothing about using a water saver on the shower nozzle - we simply let the water run and our grey tank overfilled in a hurry.

"Have you cleared the
septic tank yet? ...Dear..."

As new RVers, we received a thorough instruction from our dealer, however, our memory of each detail faded as soon as we reached our campsite. Since this was fresh shower water, I decided to drain a little on the ground until we could visit the dump station - good plan, except I pulled the wrong lever. Yes, I closed the valve in a hurry and spent the next 10 minutes trying to clean up residue left from our black water tank. Thank heavens we were only in the RV for about 12 hours and this tank was almost empty. As a co-pilot I decided then and there to become familiar with this procedure along with all the others, even though I don't have the "pleasure" of performing this task very often.

RVers who follow and understand a few basic rules of operation will find RV marine-style sanitary systems give years of satisfactory service.

Problem: Most toilets have a scissor-like trap in the toilet bowl neck that closes when a pedal or lever releases it. Occasionally, when there's insufficient water in the bowl before flushing, paper frequently becomes caught in its path and gets packed under the seal. Sometimes granules of non-dissolved toilet chemicals also get stuck around this rim and force the trap open a few millimetres. If the water won't stay in the bowl you have a problem. The trap no longer closes completely and tank gases enter the RV and the seal dries out.

Solution: Instruct all occupants, visitors included, that the paper must be floating before flushing.

Removing the packed residue under the trap is sometimes possible by working a home-made right-angle tool around the seal. Try to construct your adapter without sharp edges to avoid damaging the rubber seal. In severe cases, RV mechanics must completely remove the toilet to fix this problem.

Using a heavy spray nozzle (connected to a water hose from the outside) to flush the toilet neck along the partially opened scissor valve is another trick that sometimes dislodges any residue collected around the seal.

Spraying with silicone helps keep the seal pliable. However, if RVers leave this irritating problem uncorrected, replacing the dried seal can become a major repair job.

Purchasing a new seal by itself is not always possible either. Frequently, a new seal is part of an expensive kit that includes the gears. On one occasion we found that it was more economical to replace our entire toilet at a sale price than to purchase the package of replacement parts. John and I also learned this lesson the expensive way - we replaced two toilets and one set of gears during our first six years. So remember - if water drains from the bowl, attend to the problem immediately. It will save you big bucks!

Special RV toilet paper breaks up easily in RV holding tanks but it is more expensive. Several less costly household brands of biodegradable one-ply tissue work equally as well in the marine toilet system. If you travel in the U.S. you can buy some one-ply toilet paper with 1,000 sheets per roll (this is equivalent to just about three rolls of regular size rolls; storing one roll takes less space than three). The paper is biodegradable, economical and easy to store.

Some manufacturers suggest using a tissue digester in their product line for those RVers who have tissue build-up inside their black water tank.

To effectively deodorize and break up waste add a small amount of "blue/green stuff" (liquid holding tank chemicals) to the tank. Whether you choose a deodorant solution, a formaldehyde or enzyme-based product, these chemicals come in many easy-to-use formulas, from liquids to powder to pills.

Mix a small amount with one gallon of water to your empty black water tank. Add a touch more at the 1/2 level mark. Your tank always remains fresh this way and you stretch the amount of chemicals used. Stock up on these costly products while they are on sale at RV supply stores.

Because most RVers dump before these reservoirs are completely full, we usually reduce the amount of chemical solution recommended by manufacturers for a 40-gallon tank. But, try to avoid emptying your tank if it's less than 1/2 mark level - the added pressure of liquid in the tank gives a cleaner flush.

Movement of the liquid aids in keeping the tank clean, especially the black water tank with its added chemicals. Periodically, when we expect to have sewer hookups at our next stop, I add a double dose of solution and lots of water before we change destinations. The agitation caused by driving ensures that our tank is squeaky clean when we reach our park. If you follow this practice, remember that each gallon of water adds 10 pounds to your vehicle weight.

Using grey water tank disinfectant freshens your drains and tanks but how much and how often you use grey water chemicals depends on the degree of food residue in your kitchen sink drains. John and I leave our grey valve open when we're camped with sewer hookups. If you keep yours closed until the tank is full before dumping it, you will probably use more chemicals than we do.

> *Wise RVers will not use home remedies in their holding tanks. These solutions may control odours, but they could damage sensitive components, seals and valves. Also, most home brews do not kill all the bacteria that can grow in your tanks.*

Flushing your black water tank every once in a while is beneficial. Dump the contents, rinse tank with a hose or specialized rinsing wands or a back-flush attachment, close valves, add solutions and water to the 3/4 level. If possible, take a short drive and drain your tank again. Close valves and add small amounts of solutions and your tank will be fresh and ready for use. Although you don't have to thoroughly rinse your tank every time you dump, flushing and treating your tank is extremely important if your RV will be sitting idle for an extended period of time.

There is considerable controversy about the pros and cons of grey water draining on the ground. When water from the sink and shower doesn't sit in the tank, it has no smell to it. However, if it drains directly into the ground, environmentalists say that the earth becomes contaminated. At the park that we go to each summer many residents are seasonal. (Seasonal is when the RV is parked on a site for an extended - sometimes years - period of time.) The owners recommend that RVers dig a hole and drain the grey water into the ground. It doesn't matter where you are, never, never, never do this with your black water, even if your neighbours do.

Camping directories, tourist offices, welcome centres and even Chamber of Commerce offices should be able to direct you to a proper dumping facility when needed in an emergency.

The gauge indicators inside most RVs are frequently inaccurate. This doesn't necessarily mean paper or residue has stuck to the measure device - believe it or not - some recorders are so sensitive that they never provide correct readings. For instance, the indicator on our previous motorhome was only accurate when the tank reached 1/4 full. On this motorhome, even after servicing, our gauges continue to be less than satisfactory.

> It's okay to leave your grey water open when you're hooked up to sewer. If you keep it closed and the tank overflows, stale water will back up in your shower. It will smell like something died and everything you store in your shower will be saturated with the same foul odour.

However, because it's easy to see if the black tank is full through the toilet neck and the grey tanks overflow into the shower, it really isn't a big problem when gauges read incorrectly.

There are many things that will help you keep your sanitation system working the way it is supposed to work. The first is to always use biodegradable products in your black tank. Placing used toilet tissue in a separate container rather than the toilet is an un-hygienic practice and isn't necessary with today's holding tank solutions. The paper completely dissolves when deposited in the proper commercial tank chemicals. If one product isn't satisfactory, try another - the choice is extensive.

One RVing friend prefers to use facial tissue in lieu of toilet paper because the facial tissue is softer and colour co-ordinated to her bathroom. She feels that because it is softer it will disintegrate faster. This is not true. When wet, facial tissue clumps into a sodden ball and shouldn't even be used in your home toilet let alone your marine toilet.

During a Thetford Sanitation seminar, the staff explained pointers on maintaining your sanitation system. They stressed the importance of not using any petroleum products (Vaseline, WD-40, etc.) on sewage valves. Using these products over time will swell the valves and dry them out. Instead of correcting the problem of a sticky valve, petroleum products add to the difficulty. Thetford toilet manufacturers recommend using only a silicone-based spray to loosen a sticky valve. It was also suggested that a drain valve lubricant be added periodically to the tanks. The lubricant conditions from the inside.

> When camped in a park with sewer hookups always keep your black (toilet) water valve closed. If it's left open, the liquids drain away and the solids collect on the bottom and clog your sewer hose. This, too, is a messy task to clean up if you do it yourself and costly if you have an RV repair station correct your problem. We found this out the hard way!

Trying to connect the sewer hose to some standard adapters is at times impossible. One solution is to fill a container with hot, soapy water then place the end of your sewer hose in the water. While it is soaking, lubricate the bottom of a wine bottle with liquid soap and coat the hose attachments with liquid soap, as well. When the sewer hose is warm, stretch it over the bottle, remove the bottle and connect the hose to the fixtures. Some of the new-style adapters have easy and quick connectors for sewer hoses.

There are many handy sewer attachments on the market that provide an excellent air-tight seal when your hose is connected to the park receptacle. In most campgrounds it is mandatory to add a black rubber donut (available from any RV store and the majority of campgrounds) between the hose and the PVC pipe to achieve an air-tight seal. Since these black donuts are inexpensive, pick up a couple and don't be caught without one. Not being able to use sewer connections because you can't comply with city ordinance can be very frustrating.

When camped with sewer hookups, it's easy to frequently dump and, during these times, we find our entire system works more efficiently if we use an excess amount of water with each toilet flush. But, when we're only using holding tanks and must conserve liquids, we find using our toilet spray hose in conjunction with a round-styled toilet brush efficiently cleans the bowl and neck without excess water. However, always keep a small amount of water in the bowl or the seal will dry out.

Though most RVs have showers on board, some RVers prefer to use park or campground showers. Before heading off to the shower, check to see if you need coins to activate the water. Carrying coins and shampoo bottles from your RV to the shower can be awkward and creative RVers find numerous ways to transport these supplies. One lady we know refills trial-size bottles for each member of her family and, if these mini-containers are left behind, there's no waste. Another finds that the removable cutlery basket from her dishwasher is a convenient tote to carry shampoos and bath gel to park showers.

There are so many different ways to do things when RVing that there is no right or wrong way. Talk to other RVers - it's surprising how many ingenious solutions RVers come up with to make life easier.

The bathroom might be the smallest area in your RV but it can ensure that your travel is more comfortable, especially when you don't have to worry about the cleanliness of public washrooms. Take care of facilities in this room and it will return years of satisfactory service. ■

Winter Storage - Spring Ready

"Personally...we use sparkling water for our battery!"

Winterizing an RV or taking it out of storage and getting it ready to hit the road is a big job. You may want to hire a professional to do everything but the cleaning. However, the following tips will guide the do-it-yourselfer through each step.

John and I go south each winter, therefore, we don't winterize our unit. However, we asked many RVers what they do and the following is an synopsis of their procedures.

Putting Your RV In Hibernation

All lines must be free of water to avoid freezing. Lines can be cleared by blowing compressed air through the system. Though some people swear by this method, it's not foolproof. Unfortunately, some water residue will remain.

To withstand our Canadian winters the best method of clearing the lines is to add antifreeze to the system. Most RVers bypass the fresh and hot water tanks when adding non-toxic RV antifreeze.

The first step is to clean and flush all tanks. Add antifreeze to your fresh water tank or, using the bypass, directly to the water lines. Starting with the tap the farthest from the pump, turn each one on (don't forget the shower) until you see antifreeze flowing out of the faucet. Turn off faucets and flush the toilet, then pour some windshield-wiper antifreeze down the toilet and through the drains to the grey tank.

You can purchase an easy-to-install bypass kit from your RV dealer. To save money on the cost of RV antifreeze, you can also install a second valve. This valve fits between the fresh water tank and the water pump. There is a short piece of hose that is placed directly in the antifreeze bottle and when the pump is turned on, it pulls the antifreeze through the water lines when you open the taps. See your dealer for details.

Note: If you are going to use your RV in cold weather and your tanks are not in a heated compartment, always add wind-shield-wiper antifreeze to both grey and black tanks after dumping. Windshield-wiper fluid is less expensive than RV antifreeze. A word of caution - **never** add windshield-wiper fluid to your **fresh** water tank - windshield-wiper fluid is poisonous.

Another thing to remember - if you're winter camping and you don't have heat strips for your hoses, do not connect them to campground hookups. Either carry water on board in jugs or, if your fresh water tank is heated, fill the tank, disconnect the hose and store it away. This also applies to your sewer hose. Wait until your grey and black water tanks are filled, then connect your hose to dump. Hoses that aren't heated will freeze and split open.

Clean, check and charge your battery. Top up your batteries with distilled water. If you don't plan on using your motorhome over the winter months, remove the battery and store it some-where where it will stay cool, but not below freezing. (If your battery gets too warm, it'll discharge).

Thoroughly clean the inside and out of your RV. After clean-ing and turning the fridge and freezer off, prop open the door to eliminate odours and stop mildew from growing. Leave several open boxes of baking soda inside the fridge. Cover all external vents and openings with tinfoil to stop pests from making a nest. Don't forget to protect the air conditioner with a cover.

Close all drapes and blinds to prevent the sun's rays from deteriorating and fading fabric. Reduce air pressure on the tires and jack up the RV, if possible, to extend tire life.

> *Installing the new-style vent covers that allow air circulation will eliminate the stale, closed up smell of an unoccupied RV without letting in rain, snow or pests.*

Keep gas tanks full to prevent condensation from forming. Turn off your propane tanks and make sure that the place where you are storing your RV is level - it relieves stress on the frame.

Spring into Action

At the first hint of spring RVing Canadians, especially those who weathered our blustery winter, are anxious to get on the road. It's really difficult to hold back the desire to load the RV and take off for parts unknown.

However, while we may have been active over the winter, our RVs have been hibernating, some under a blanket of snow. Although these units are made to withstand all sorts of weather, they do need a bit of TLC to keep them in tip-top shape. RVs, after all, are investments and a little bit of elbow grease and preventive maintenance each spring could save you hundreds of dollars in costly on-the-road repairs.

Now that winter is over, it's time for spring-cleaning, RV style. To nip potential problems in the bud, wise RVers set up a simple maintenance and clean-up schedule. First of all, open all the windows and let in some of that fresh spring breeze to get rid of that musty, closed up smell. Do a visual check of connections, propane, water hoses, pipes and valves. Make sure that none are cracked or corroded.

Look behind the fridge and inspect the area for any signs of mice, birds, spider webs and any other blockages. Clean the area. If there are any signs of rust on the coils, lightly rub the surface with a dry steel wool pad.

While your coach is airing out, check thoroughly for any sign of water seepage on the walls, floors and ceiling. A build-up of snow may have weakened the roof.

Water stains could show up on the walls or rust stains may be apparent on the roof frame. If your roof looks even the slightest bit droopy there is probably a leak and it will need fixing. If the leak is extensive it may be time to call in the professionals.

While you're on the roof, again check for signs of mice and birds. Remove all nests and other debris. If your air conditioner is leaking, check the caulking around the opening. To repair, just scrape away the caulking, wash and rinse away the residue, let dry and apply your sealant. If you still find water leaking around the air conditioner after resealing it is probably condensation and you should call your dealer for advice.

Take a walk around the outside of your RV. Check all handles and hardware to make sure each one works properly. Look in every nook and cranny for mice or birds and other pests (especially in your storage pods). Examine the skin of your RV. If you see a bit of surface rust, don't panic. This is a fairly common occurrence after being in storage. Usually a quick buff with sandpaper and a touch-up with rust protector will remove the rust and prevent further corrosion.

Look at all the electrical connections to make sure the wires aren't cracked. If there's a chalky-looking substance on the connectors, it's just a residue left courtesy of winter and road salt. Brush it off with wire brush, steel wool or even sandpaper. Make sure that the road salt hasn't plugged any outside electrical sockets. This could cause corrosion leading to shortages. If the sockets are corroded, replace immediately. Electrical shortages may also be caused by low electrolyte levels in your battery. After cleaning the battery and connectors, top up the electrolyte levels with distilled water.

For motorized RVs, check all the parts of your engine and fluid levels before starting. Make sure that no furry little critters have taken up residence. While you're at it, check all lights (this also applies to towables).

Check all bearings and connections on tow hitches. Test the electrical connections of the brakes. Connect the brakes to an ammeter and a battery. If the ammeter doesn't register amperage, the magnet isn't getting any energy and will have to be replaced. (This test should be done at least once, maybe twice a year and, if you don't want to do it yourself, take it to a professional.)

A definite must is to ensure that your tires are in tip-top shape. Inflate your tires to the maximum and check for leaks, cracks or uneven wear. (Remember to deflate them again to the proper air pressure before driving.) If you log many miles with your RV, rotate the tires annually. The next step is to wash and spray tires with a non-petroleum protective cleaner.

Now it's time to flush out the plumbing. Remember when your RV was stored for the winter and you poured antifreeze into the tanks and lines to prevent freezing? Well, it's time to purge that solution.

Partially fill your fresh water tank (it was drained last fall), and open both bypass valves, all your faucets and flush the toilet. When the water stops bubbling, the antifreeze is gone. To purge the fresh water tank, fill it about three-quarters full with warm water and add four to six ounces of chlorine bleach. Drive your RV around the block a couple of times to agitate the water and give the water tanks an extra cleaning boost. When back home, drain the tanks. Refill the tank and let the water run through the faucets until clear and chlorine free. Refill the tank with water. If you choose, also put in a very weak solution of chlorine bleach (1/2 teaspoon per 10 gallons of water) to purify the water.

If water is pooling around plumbing lines and fixtures or you find damp spots by your water pump, there is a leak. It may be a loose clamp that just needs tightening or it could be a damaged hose or pipe that needs replacing.

With all the flushing and draining, your black and grey water tanks are also being cleaned. Don't forget to check the holding tanks for leaks. The best indicator of a problem is an unpleasant "backed-up sewer" smell. Even if you can't detect any odours, get down on your hands and knees and feel around the toilet for water. Examine the trap and pour water down into the hole. If the water comes back up into the bowl, your pipe is blocked. If it's still cold outside and your toilet system was properly cleaned before storage, the pipe could just be frozen and you'll have to wait for a thaw to retest the trap. If the blockage is still there, try adding an extra dose of toilet chemical, let sit for a while and gently scrub the pipe with a round toilet brush. When everything "moves" as expected, clean and disinfect the bathroom and add grey and black water solutions to the appropriate tanks.

> *If your taps or flush mechanism seem stiff, lubricate with a silicone-based product because products containing petroleum (such as Vaseline or WD-40), will disintegrate rubber.*

Check all propane lines and valves for not-visible-to-the-naked-eye cracks or pinhole leaks. First run a pressure test - turn on your propane and if the pressure is low, you probably have a leak.

Now do a soap bubble test. Mix liquid dish soap with a bit of water. Take a soft toothbrush and brush the soapy mixture all over the hoses, line, valves and gas regulator. If bubbles appear you've found your leak. Turn the propane off until problem is corrected. Do not do a patch repair to propane leaks - **replace** any faulty lines, hoses and valves. All propane connections, the burner flue and fridge coils should be inspected by a service mechanic with S-4 propane certification.

Continue with a thorough spring cleaning. Sweep away any cobwebs and dead bugs. Sprinkle your carpets (and upholstery) with the appropriate freshener and let it sit before vacuuming away. While you are waiting for the carpet freshener to take hold, remove dust and use a no-rinse cleaner on the inside of cupboards and closets. Clean the counters, fixtures and appliances. Don't forget to check for mice and birds (in every area) and give the carpet a thorough vacuum.

Apply lemon oil to all your wood cabinetry. Not only does this give your interior a special gleam, it helps preserve the wood. Check all door handles and hinges for stiffness or looseness and lubricate or tighten accordingly.

Shine up the surface of your appliances, your sink, taps and counter-top with a vinegar and water solution. For that extra sparkle, buff all appliances, sinks and faucets with used fabric softener sheets. These sheets are anti-static and do an excellent job of cleaning the TV, VCR, stereo fronts and computer. Before tackling the windows, take down the curtains and check the window seals for leaks. Wash the curtains and wipe the blinds with a no-rinse cleaner. For the final touch, clean the windows.

Next, wash the interior and exterior of the fridge, turn it on (it was turned off and the door left open for winter storage). If you haven't already done it, do the dish soap and water test on all fridge propane connections. To avoid overworking the fridge motor, let it run on medium-low for a day or two before loading it up with supplies. (A tip for travelling: try to have most of your food cold or frozen before transferring it to your RV fridge.)

Finally, wash the exterior of your RV - if you have the opportunity. Because many parks have a "no wash" policy, John and I prefer to use one of the many types of no rinse cleaners on the market. We fill a spray bottle with a mixture of the cleaner and water (manufacturer's recommendations), spray it on and simply wipe it off with a soft cloth. If your RV is really dirty, add no rinse cleaner to a bucket of water and, using a brush or a large sponge, clean the unit and dry it off with a soft cloth. No rinsing is required.

While you're doing all that exterior washing, unroll your awning and examine carefully for tears, worn spots or mildew stains. Wash the awning with an appropriate cleaner and thoroughly rinse. (Don't use abrasive and strong commercial cleaners on your awning as it may remove the water-repellent qualities of the treated fabric.) Re-apply cleaner and roll awning while wet. Leave a few minutes, unroll and rinse the solution off. It may be necessary to repeat this procedure to remove stubborn stains. This way, with a light once-over with a brush and a rinse, the dirt effortlessly washes away from both sides of the awning.

Before rerolling or patching the awning make sure it is completely dry. You can buy patching kits for awnings and, if you do see a tear or worn spot, patch immediately following the manufacturer's recommendations. When the awning is extended, your screen door can catch and tear the fabric. However, there are protectors - either a wheel-type or plastic awning saver - that fit over the corner of the door. For under two toonies and a loonie, these make a good investment.

Wash and dry every part of the awning hardware with a brush and mild soap and water solution. Lubricate and tighten all loose bolts and screws, then finish with a polish.

If you see chips in your windshield or windows, take your unit to a window repair specialist - it's free to the customer. With the techniques used to renew chipped glass, you could end up saving hundreds of dollars by avoiding the eventual cracking that will occur. Even if your deductible is $250, it will generally be waived for stone chip repairs.

You will probably develop your own routine of getting your RV ready for the road. Use these hints as a guideline and adapt them to your system. But remember, preventive maintenance is the first step to enjoying your on-the-road summer fun. And, once these necessary chores are done, you won't have to repeat them again...until the fall. But that's another story.

Enjoy your summer and we'll see you down the road! ∎

Travelling With Pets

"So...you have to bring your
lab buddies with you!"

Not all RVers have children and grandchildren but quite a few of RVers have pets. John and I always travel with our dachshunds in our motorhome and, without exception, these four-legged angels love the RV lifestyle. We have yet to encounter problems while exploring the U.S. and Mexico with our dogs on board.

There have, however, been times when our plans to stop at some state parks or the occasional private campground changed because of a "no pet" policy. John and I simply avoid these places. North America is so vast that it's impossible to see it all so we concentrate on areas where our dogs are as welcome as we. Travelling with large dogs or more than two pets (cats or dogs) may open the door to more problems.

When our pets see us getting ready to change destinations, they immediately assume their driving positions - curled up on the couch. They know another location with new smells, pet walks, sights and sounds is waiting for them to explore.

Our dogs are small but many RVers travel with large four-legged friends. Crossing either the U.S. or Mexican border is no problem if your pets receive their required annual shots, especially rabies. **Always** carry the International Statement of Health provided by your Canadian veterinarian for each pet on board with you. These regulations apply to dogs and cats - for other types of pets such as birds or fish, ask your veterinarian about border crossing regulations and restrictions.

Wise travellers also have a copy of their pet's history with them. This is particularly important if your pet has health problems or requires special medication. Make sure that all pet medications have descriptive labelling and, if possible, carry a copy of their prescriptions with you. In an emergency, it may help an unfamiliar vet diagnose your pet's problem plus, if you are delayed in returning to Canada, it's easier for the vet to refill a prescription if he/she knows what medication your pet is taking. The written prescription is also proof (if ever needed) to custom agents that you have legally acquired the medication and why it is necessary.

RVers who travel with pets do encounter one reoccurring and frustrating problem - controlling fleas. Each area of a warm climate has its own breed of annoying flea population. Some places are much worse than others but, with the regular use of an effective flea spray and pet shampoo, it is possible to keep the infestation under control. If you're in an area where your flea spray seems ineffective, visit a local vet to see what they would recommend for local conditions. Both pets and their beds require regular flea control maintenance. Don't forget to flea-proof your RV as well. There is a new flea pill available from your vet but it is relatively expensive. Administered monthly, this pill is reported to work very well controlling fleas.

John and I spend a considerable amount of time travelling in warm climates and, as much as we love it, mosquitoes love it just as much. As a result, we keep our dogs on heartworm medication for the whole year. We discovered several years ago that some brands of heartworm pills sold in Canada contain different ingredients than those sold in the southern U.S. The U.S. brands were also more costly than ours and we couldn't even buy heartworm pills in Mexico. To simplify things, four years ago we switched our dogs to a monthly pill and we now purchase the whole amount during their annual checkup in Canada.

Sometimes, at new destinations, it's difficult to find a particular brand of food or supplies that your pet particularly enjoys. Most RVers carry a back-up supply of all essentials in their RV. Unnecessary changes are not good for anyone and, after all, your pet is a valued family member and should be treated as such.

Unfortunately, pets do become lost or venture away from campsites. At times they can't remember where "mom" and "dad" parked their travelling home. RVers with animals should consider registering with a lost pet service. Subscribing to a locating service through the Good Sam RV Club or private organizations supported by your veterinarian helps a pet and its owner find each other. As a "lost pet" member, your pet wears an identification tag bearing a membership number plus a toll-free number to call. If your pet does get lost, simply call the number to record your location. With luck, the person who finds your four-legged friend will also telephone the number to report finding your pet. If all goes well, you and your "baby" can soon become travel partners again.

Our dachshunds are senior members we adopted from a show kennel. When they first came into our care they were already into their retirement years (ages 5 - 7) and, like us, they had already formed their habits. While outside for fresh air they prefer a collapsible playpen rather than be tied to a leash. Because they are small, fellow campers always want to stop, say hello and pet them. Our "children", although tiny, quickly change into very protective and ferocious guard dogs. To protect ourselves (and others) we display a sign with the words "guard dogs on duty". This lets visitors know to keep their distance and that the playpen is off limits.

Pets are loyal friends but they do need conscientious owners to take care of them. Remember that pets can't clean up after themselves plus noisy animals irritate and frighten others. Most campgrounds welcome pets but, if pet owners hope to keep it that way, cleaning up after your pets and respecting fellow RVers is mandatory. One prominently displayed sign we saw in a campground in Nova Scotia said it all, "Got a Dog? Got a Shovel? Get the Picture???"

One Arizona park we were in had an 80-site pet section. It was wonderful camping beside RVers who also had dogs or cats. Everyone understands an occasional barking dog and other pet owners are usually ready to help out if problems occur when you're temporarily away from your RV.

Another challenge when travelling with pets is trying to keep the temperature of your RV comfortable during the times when you have to leave them alone in your coach. If you leave your RV early in the morning it may be too cold to turn your air conditioner on or to open windows. Unfortunately, cool mornings frequently turn into extremely hot afternoons - especially in a closed-up RV. We discovered a solution to this dilemma when we upgraded our motorhome in 1993 and had Fan-Tastic vents installed. With these thermostat-controlled vents the interior of our unit always remains comfortable, both for us and our pets.

> *Approximately five states have a no pet policy in their state parks. RVers travelling with cats or dogs are not welcome in these campgrounds. Check campground directories or ask at welcome centres/tourist bureaus if the park you are considering accepts pets. It's apparent that non-considerate pet owners have effectively worn out their welcome (yours too) in some areas so always be a responsible pet owner. As you leave a campground ask yourself if you and your pets were welcome - if the answer is yes, then you've done your part.*

Travelling with a pet adds to the RV experience. Pets offer companionship plus provide a sense of security for RVers, although, I do have to admit, they do tie us down at times. When something comes up that excludes our dogs we board them with an animal clinic. Since our dogs are older, we prefer to leave them at a facility where a doctor is close at hand - just in case. Animal hospital boarding rates are similar to rates at kennels and it's comforting for us to know medical help is available for our "old girls".

Unfortunately, pets don't live as long as people. Since ours are seniors when they begin travelling with us, we must face the prospect of a pet becoming ill or even dying in distant places. This is a situation no one likes to think about but, if faced with this decision, we look for an animal clinic which will not only quickly send our pet to "animal heaven" but provide burial or cremation services as well.

Several years ago our 16½ year old baby became sick with pneumonia. The vet couldn't work miracles and she died. There was so much love, concern and caring in that clinic and the staff not only offered us a spot in their special cemetery behind the clinic, they also sent us a unique pet sympathy card several days later. It was a welcome and comforting touch especially since we missed our old girl very much.

Yes, travelling with pets does carry some responsibilities and restrictions. All things considered though, we would never even consider travelling without four-legged children on board. ■

More Money For Your Trade-In

No matter how much you love your present RV, there comes a time in every RVer's life when trading-in your present unit for a larger (or smaller RV) is necessary. Once you've made the decision to trade-in, getting the most value for your old unit is the top priority. Although most sellers don't go to the trouble to update or modernize an older RV, John and I did and we found the redecorating experience a rewarding challenge.

When we traded our 1983 Pace Arrow in May of 1993, she glistened. Our "Kruisin' Kastle", a renovated showpiece celebrating her 10th birthday, had served us well. Her last year was one of her finest but we had to make a big decision - do we run her for countless more miles and lose trade-in value or do we go for the brass ring?

We dreamed of the pleasure associated with driving a new 38-footer - we could feel it, we could even see it. Especially when a twin to our new "dream machine" backed into an adjoining campsite. John and I gazed in awe, envious of that beautiful motorhome and wondered if owning an RV so elegant could ever become a possibility.

We had to face facts and even though we knew it was time to replace our 32-foot Class A, we wanted her new owners to enjoy our Kruisin' Kastle as much as we did. John and I spent many hours over the winter giving her a face-lift.

To bring her interior decor into the '90s, we recovered the furniture in a soft green upholstery fabric. Covering existing fabric wall panels plus creating two extra sofa cushions added a comfy touch.

Using a mint and emerald green colour scheme, the kitchen, bath and bedroom received an elegant uplift with new wallpaper (including inside of the cupboards and the air conditioner covers). New bedspreads, mini-blinds, curtains and valences completed her interior decor. We used pale blue fabric to update the existing front windshield drapery and lace, cafe-style curtains provided a finishing touch to the living room. We then replaced her worn carpet from front to back with an easy-to-clean, quality vinyl floor highlighted by emerald green carpet runners. Each of these inexpensive modifications enhanced the value and appearance of our 10-year-old coach.

Finishing the wood cabinets with a generous dose of lemon oil finalized and accented her new image. All things considered, the inside of our reliable older RV was ready to move into another decade.

Next step was the outside. Replacing old caulking on the roof and around several windows ensured she was leak free. Heavy-duty boat cleaner removed every trace of oxidization from her fibreglass skin. We completed her make-over with a coat of protective boat wax, plus a once-over of chrome polish and tire shine. Our Kruisin' Kastle was ready to show off her sparkling image at the dealer's lot. We were certain that her attractive appearance would quickly attract new owners. Hope they love her as much as we did.

We learned a lot from this experience and, although it was time consuming to modify an old RV, it really wasn't too difficult. RVers with even the minimum of wallpapering knowledge can use the same principles in both a house or an RV. The only difference is that in confined RV areas there's more cutting around corners. Vinyl-to-vinyl adhesive, designed to secure border surfaces, works exceptionally well as a medium for sticking wallpaper on to covered RV wallboards.

To make sure that we received the best trade-in value possible we took along recent exterior and interior photos at our first negotiation meeting with the dealer as well as a list of all modifications, additions and important maintenance repairs for the previous three years.

For instance, we replaced our tires with "F"-rated Michelins, our three-way eight cubic foot Dometic refrigerator was new and so were the radiator, alternator, batteries and much more. Each item increased the trade-in value of our motorhome and, when presenting our resale unit this way, the dealer knew exactly what we had and could offer us a realistic trade-in value.

Although you may not want to completely redecorate, before you take your unit in for an appraisal, clean both the interior and exterior of your RV. If you are still using your unit, clean and organize the cupboards and closets. Make sure that the bathroom and all appliances are spotless. Rearrange your countertop so that it doesn't look cluttered (and smaller) and, while you're at it, move any old magazine or newspaper collections out of sight.

Rent a carpet cleaner and shampoo the rugs and upholstery. Wash (or dust) the walls, floors, blinds and curtains. Use window cleaner on the windows, mirrors, glass doors and faucets.

Do minor repairs. Remember, the better your unit looks, the more trade-in value it will command.

If you are trading a motorized RV, have the engine tuned. Replace spark plugs, etc., if needed. A few dollars spent before an appraisal could translate into hundreds of dollars extra. ∎

On The Road

"Didn't you know...RVers and birds both migrate at the same time."

Though travelling in your RV is a great way to spend a vacation, there are some points you should take note of before you set out. When John and I began extensive RVing 11 years ago we were looking for perpetual summer sunshine. We'd been holidaying during November and March in Florida for several years and it was always beautiful and warm. With retirement approaching, we couldn't find any reason why we couldn't enjoy the warm sunshine all year round.

Most areas in Canada and the U.S. have several outstanding seasons, unfortunately, they also have snow, cold, rain or extreme heat and none, not even the sunny south, has a perfect year-round climate.

We did, however, find as close to perfect as you could get when we discovered the perpetual warmth south of Guadalajara, Mexico. At a place called Lake Chapala, we enjoyed heavenly temperatures hovering around the 21 to 28 Celsius mark (70 to 80 Fahrenheit). Unfortunately, to enjoy this weather, we had to drive an extra 1,000-kilometres below the U.S. border so, for the past few years, we have been roaming and exploring the U.S. southern states.

RVers searching for memorable travels must be flexible and ready for anything. That means packing a substantial number of clothes for any type of climate. Along with your bathing suits, shorts and sandals include a few winter items, such as jackets and sweaters. Although it's possible to follow the sun, sometimes the weather doesn't co-operate and, even in the sun belt, temperatures can fall. You will also need the appropriate clothing for Canada's spring and fall temperatures.

Autumn has to be one of the most beautiful times to travel, especially in eastern Canada and the north-eastern states where the whole area transforms into a vibrant, fiery collage of colours.

When John and I travel, we only drive for one short day (approximately six hours) and then stop for three to seven days to explore our surroundings. Besides staying rested en route and taking in the sights along the way, we enjoy the added advantage of a fall season that lasts at least six weeks. Travelling this way is relaxing and the journey is every bit as pleasant as the stay at our winter-stopping spot. To increase our enjoyment we try to use secondary roads when it's possible. Not only is the scenery more interesting than on the fast-paced major highway and interstate systems, the traffic is lighter and driving is more relaxed.

RVers should be wary when in the U.S. during the spring season. This is the prime season for tornados, violent thunder-storms, flooding (especially flash flooding) and even the occasional and unexpected snowstorm. We always stayed tuned to local radio and TV stations for constant weather-watch updates.

If a tornado is imminent, get out of your vehicle and go to a low-lying area such as a ditch. If you are near an overpass with girders, climb as high as possible inside the overpass to get out of the tornado's path. During a tornado, cars, trucks, semis and RVs plus every other object in its path are tossed around like twigs in a brisk breeze. Observe the warnings, however, be thankful if they are overstated.

Our education never stops and this includes learning about unfamiliar weather patterns. One spring afternoon in Iowa we were watching TV and the continual reporting of a tornado watch listed by counties was on the corner of the picture. This was a new experience for us and, when the park manager knocked on our door to warn us of the watch, we had to ask what that meant. He advised us to evacuate our motorhome and come to the park's reinforced clubhouse/restaurant. RVers and their children and assorted pets all gathered in our temporary refuge. Only then did we learn that a watch preceded a warning when reporting weather conditions. If a warning is on the screen, take cover immediately. Our evacuation experience wasn't a false alarm - a tornado touched down 1/4 of a mile away.

The tornado incident showed us that we needed a more complete understanding of strange weather patterns as well as knowing what action to take. Keeping a special weather radio on hand helps to keep on top of the complete storm picture. We discovered that regular radio and TV stations also report dangerous county weather activity.

Before this incident, as the primary navigator, I completely ignored county markings on road maps. I really never cared what county I was in as I had no plan to pay their taxes or apply to vote. Believe me, after this frightening experience, both John and I became much more conscientious of travel during adverse weather conditions.

One additional reason for being aware of county markings is that radio announcers not only report what county is under warning, they also report where the weather is coming from and where it is headed. Knowing the path of a weather pattern helps you to make an educated decision about whether or not to keep on driving.

These same DJs suggest helpful tips and precautions travellers should take during specific weather situations, including flash floods or even earthquakes. The radio also reports accidents or delays on the highway, broken down by county markings. Suddenly we realized that these insignificant map markings are very important to our immediate travel plans.

As RVers, we have the privilege to experience the joys of all four seasons, plus we have the option to shorten our stays in the not so pleasant locations. ■

Planning Your Route

"What do you mean...Florida again!"

Much like one unit won't be perfect for every RVer, there is also more than one correct way to plan your trip. Travellers find almost as many ways to plan a vacation getaway as there are RVers on the road. Some like the freedom to stop when they feel the urge, others want each detail checked, double-checked and verified weeks in advance - although most RVers find a common ground between these two extremes.

RVers who don't feel comfortable planning a vacation may prefer to use the trip routing service offered by many of the large RV clubs. CAA (Canadian Automobile Association) and several other auto clubs provide this service for their members.

There are also several computer programs available to help travellers with route planning or you can check your bookstores and public library for information on trip preparation.

Seasoned RVers are aware that, during holiday weekends, campgrounds in Canada are extremely busy. In U.S. sun country, the busy periods are from January to March and spaces in

RV parks are quickly booked to capacity. Even RVers who like to travel with unrestricted freedom and without confining plans make reservations for busy times in high season.

In our family, John does all the trip planning. If I want to visit a particular spot, I make my wishes known and he fits it into the schedule. When John plans our trip he plots a route between our two main destinations using a descriptive atlas plus a Rand McNally Dist-O-Map (automatic mileage dialler) to estimate driving distances.

Next, he looks for interesting stops along our route using the atlas plus various campground directories listing all of North America . He also takes notes of places that are promoted in the directories by each park and from travel articles in RV magazines.

As we like to limit our driving to a maximum of 480 km per day, John decides where the best stop-over places are and how long we'll stay to do some sightseeing. We like to relax between driving days which contributes to a healthier and less stressful trip.

Once we reach our destination and after setting up camp, we fine-tune our research of the area by talking to the park staff about must-see places. We also visit local tourist bureaus and welcome centres.

Our military training to follow a schedule is deeply ingrained into our make-up. If we arrive at an unreserved campground and we can't stay because the park is full or for some other reason, both of us become irritated and words which shouldn't be even thought of are spoken. The air inside our motorhome takes on a vibrant shade of blue as we try to decide where to go next. Neither of us works well in an impulse situation.

However, many RVers prefer to travel without reservations and stop at attractions when they see something interesting. In our case we settle into a campsite, unhook the car and then explore the attractions. We also don't like to camp or stop in unprotected areas.

Because the rate of crime is high at some rest areas, many

truck stops have redesigned their stations to accommodate and encourage RVers to stop for the night. The Flying J, Ambest and '76 Truck Stops (among others) have put out the welcome mat for RVers. Along with fuel (gas, diesel and propane) and mechanical service, most have restaurants, convenience stores, restrooms with showers and a safe place to park for the night. Many have dump stations as well. At some of the '76 Truck Stops and Ambest chains, there is a separate designated RV parking area. In the centres without this feature, RVs park with the trucks. It doesn't cost anything to park in these areas overnight and they come in handy when you wish to take a break from driving or get off the road for the night. Some restaurants also allow overnight parking but, before you pull off somewhere for the night, ask the owners or managers if it's allowed.

Sometimes provincial and national parks, community campgrounds and conservation areas plus state and Bureau of Land Management parks in the U.S. may be more economical than private campgrounds. Listings are available from welcome centres and tourist bureaus. These are all worth checking out to compare prices, especially if you're travelling on a budget. Ask if the site price includes the day-use fee or if that fee is extra. The day-use fee adds tremendously to your camping costs.

While at the welcome centres, information booths or tourist bureau offices, check to see what out-of-the-way places are waiting for you to discover. Ask if there are any discount coupon books for the area. With a minimum amount of planning, RV travel can be the most exciting time of your life.

Keep your timetable flexible! Frequently, our most interesting stops have been on the advice of other RVers. Find time to visit and investigate the places where you camp - your stopovers will take on a whole new meaning.

Discovering unique and colourful places adds another dimension to your journey. We frequently find several ideas for places to visit from local newspapers at our stopovers. Visiting these places are not only fun, they're also educational.

Don't try to, nor expect to see everything the first visit. It's more interesting if you save some experiences for return trips. It's natural for new RVers on holidays or beginning their retirement to try to see it all "yesterday".

Don't worry if you get lost. Find a safe place to pull over, take a deep breath and examine the map before continuing.

A good atlas is a necessity and it should list counties, highway and interstate exit numbers, major city maps and provinces and states in alphabetical order rather than in regional order. ∎

Anything to Declare?

"As soon as I told him we bought this in the US, he got real friendly!"

Although we may consider our RV to be our home, when crossing a border, RVs come under the same rules as cars and that means that custom agents do not need a search warrant to enter and search an RV. Just because you have nothing to declare doesn't mean the next border crossing won't result in a complete inspection of your unit.

When approaching the inspection station, be calm and take off sun glasses so that the agent can look into your eyes. Always be polite and remember the Golden Rule - treat officials as you want to be treated, with respect. Answer each question but don't get smart or attempt to be "funny". Also, don't provide too much information - keep your response short, to the point and pertinent to only the questions asked.

Because of Canada's health coverage regulations, all Canadian residents must have a permanent "home" address located in one of our provinces or territories. Therefore, RVers must be ready to prove the length of time they were in the U.S.

Presenting gas or toll-bridge receipts helps verify where you have travelled and how long you have been out of the country.

Although the agent inputs licence numbers into the computer as vehicles pull up to a custom's station, they are mainly looking for outstanding traffic tickets and warrants.

When entering the U.S., there's a possibility that U.S. immigration agents will ask for proof of permanent Canadian residency and information regarding any property owned in Canada or ask you to produce a phone or utility bill. The agents are merely trying to determine if, as an RVer, you will be returning to Canada after your getaway.

> *Even if you spend most of the year in your RV, do not admit or brag about being a fulltimer or that your RV is your only home, especially to an immigration or custom officer.*

Revenue Canada is aware that the price of acquisitions is steadily increasing and that many travellers prefer to buy items some place other than home - even if the item in question is not a bargain. As a result, in June of 1995, personal declaration amounts were substantially increased.

To ensure that you know what is or isn't duty-free, either pick up a copy of the I Declare booklet from any custom's office - check the blue pages in the phone book under Revenue Canada, or call 1-800-461-9999 to order the free information booklet.

Personal Exemptions

• If you are out of the country for less than 24 hours, you are not eligible for a duty-free exemption. After 24 hours, the personal declaration amount is $50 Cdn., and **does not** include tobacco and/or alcohol. If your purchases exceed $50, you cannot claim your personal exemption and must pay duty on the **total** amount of your purchases.

- During cross-border visits longer than 48 hours, you are allowed $200 Cdn., including tobacco and/or alcohol, with no restrictions on how many times you use this allowable deduction. You must, however, have all purchases with you.
- After a seven-day (or more absence), the exemption rises to $500 Cdn., including alcohol and/or tobacco. Just recently the time restriction has been lifted and you can now use this exemption **any time** that you are absent from Canada for seven days or more. This exemption does not include items and gifts sent separately but, it does include gifts carried in your luggage.

To calculate the number of days you're away, count the day of return - the time (hour) isn't important - and don't include your day of departure.

You cannot combine the exemptions, nor can you use part of your exemption and carry it over to the next time you're absent. So, if you only spend $100 on your 48 hour exemption, the remainder ($100) cannot be applied to the $200 exemption the next time you are out of the country. Be advised that two (or more) people cannot pool their personal exemptions together.

> For example - if you are away for more than seven days and have a purchase item worth $1,000, you can't add your two exemptions of $500 each to equal $1,000. In this case, you would be allowed one $500 personal exemption on the item. The next $300 will be assessed at an eight percent (8 percent) flat rate and the balance (in this case $200) will be charged regular duties (at time of printing, four percent) plus GST (no PST is charged).

Gifts and awards carried with you must be declared as part of your exemption. Gifts can be mailed duty-free and tax-free to Canada, however, each one must be less than $60 Cdn. in value and cannot include tobacco and/or alcohol. Gifts over $60 will cost the recipient regular duties on excess amounts.

Tobacco and Alcohol

Tobacco and alcohol are duty-free and included in the $200 and $500 personal exemption category but not for the 24-hour/$50 declarations. Travellers over the age requirements of the province or territory where they enter Canada are allowed a total of 200 cigarettes **and** 50 cigars or cigarillos **and** 400 (2-lb.) tobacco sticks **and** 400 (2-lb.) grams of tobacco. For amounts greater than this, add current duties plus applicable provincial taxes to the overall cost. Depending on the province or territory, some limits do apply.

Canadians can bring any amounts of acceptable goods into Canada as long as they are prepared to pay import duties, excise tax (where applicable) plus GST on all items declared over your personal exemption. And, even though we now have "free trade" and some duty charges have been reduced or eliminated, import duties still apply to a wide variety of purchases.

> *Legal age of the person purchasing tobacco and/or alcohol is determined on provincial or territorial laws where you REENTER the country, not on your home province laws.*

Those meeting the age eligibility can declare 1.14 litres (40 ounces) of wine **or** liquor **or** 24 x 355 ml (8.5 litres/12 ounces) cans **or** bottles of beer **or** ale. You may bring in more than the exempted allotment but, again, you have to pay duty, provincial levies and applicable taxes. There are limits to how much you can bring into the country.

One time, because I forgot to check the regulations before arriving at the border, we were carrying too much alcohol. We had wine and beer on board. I found out that it's not "and", it should have been wine or beer. When asked, I told them the truth and didn't run into any problems - we had a choice of paying the hefty duty fee or pouring the wine down the drain. I chose the drain because the duties were too excessive.

Y-38 Cards

I'm always apprehensive as we drive up to a border crossing, even if we didn't buy any declarable items. But, when Canadians are informed and know in advance what to expect, their crossing should be uneventful. Most custom officers allow a verbal declaration but, by law, officers can demand a written declaration for all items. If asked, don't complain, just fill out the form.

Travellers using other forms of transportation such as an airplane or bus should always expect to give a written declaration at the custom's check-point.

If you're carrying valuable items with serial numbers, such as cameras and sporting goods, fill out an Identification of Articles for Temporary Exportation (Y-38 wallet card) before you leave Canada. These cards can be filled out at the border. Custom agents will record a complete description of the item, including the make, model and serial number, and list the information on the Y-38 card. The card should be carried with you any time you cross the border. Without the card, custom officers may determine that you purchased the item in the U.S. and can charge you duty.

If the items are mounted in an RV (TVs, VCRs, air conditioners, etc.), it may be necessary to present your unit for inspection. In all cases, you must prove that these personal items and RV accessories were a Canadian purchase. Carrying the original receipt is an alternative way to prove your ownership.

When we purchased our RV we asked the dealer to record each appliance and all accessories included in our purchase on the bill of sale. This way we only need Y-38 cards for any extras we have on board.

Jewellery

It's always better to leave expensive jewellery at home. However, when taking pieces across the border, bring along a photo, a written appraisal and a bill of sale (or, if previously imported, carry the custom's receipt). When jewellery that has been taken out of the country is altered in any way (new setting, replacement stone, etc.), it is subject to the same duties as if it was a newly purchased item. All modified "new" jewellery should be declared in full, regardless if it was originally purchased in Canada.

Weapons

If you plan to transport a firearm across the border, ask for the brochure Importing A Firearm or Weapon into Canada. The brochure explains all restrictions in detail. Rules change in each province/territory, depending on hunting season so asking questions before arriving at the border eliminates surprises. Importing explosives, fireworks, ammunition and similar items may need authorization as well as a permit.

Defense accessories such as pepper spray and Mace are classed as weapons - declare these items. An RVing friend recently paid costly fines for not disclosing this information.

Drugs

If you're carrying prescription drugs, have the original bottle or even photocopies of all prescriptions on board. It could prevent problems on both sides of the border - especially with the Canadian and American zero drug tolerance policies.

Food and Plants

Everyday groceries carried in a self-contained RV aren't usually questioned. Even though the import limits on meat, dairy products and fresh fruits and vegetables are very generous for personal use, the costs of these items are considered part of your personal exemption if travelling by car. Full details are listed in the *I Declare* booklet.

Before planning to transport plants into Canada, they must be inspected by an agricultural agent. For more information on plant inspections, contact a district office of Agriculture and Agri-Food, Canada's food production and inspection branch.

> *Always check with the Registrar of Imported Vehicles to see if your vehicle of choice is acceptable before you finalize any purchase.*

Importing a Vehicle

If you wish to import a vehicle into Canada, call the federal agency of the Department of Transportation (1-800-511-7755) and the Registrar of Imported Vehicles (1-800-333-0558) before making a purchase. One point many travellers may not realize is that Canadians cannot drive a U.S. licensed rental or borrowed vehicle for personal use into Canada - even for a temporary period.

All vehicles (including your motorized RV) purchased in the U.S. will be subject to duties, excise tax and GST plus a Canadian certification fee of $210 Cdn. The certification of compliance is done at the border by Department of Transportation officers. Importers have 45 days to update their imported vehicle to Canadian standards. After paying all the duties, etc., you must register your vehicle when you get home. You then pay a registration and licensing fee plus PST.

If your vehicle is manufactured anywhere other than Canada and the U.S., even if has been purchased in either two of those countries, an eight percent import duty on the full amount is charged. Under the free trade agreement, only vehicles of the current model year (other than those of Canadian or U.S. manufactured origin) can be brought into the country. Check to see what the model year is before buying.

> For example - the model year usually changes in the fall so, if you bought a 1996 European manufactured car in November of 1996, you could not import the vehicle. In November, 1996, the current model year only includes foreign vehicles manufactured for 1997.

Maintenance

Any vehicle maintenance that is done when out of Canada is charged hefty duties as well as GST. And, although "I didn't know!" may well be true, it is not an acceptable excuse. Ignorance and words won't help you avoid the high cost of duties or taxes assessed at the border. Revenue Canada custom agents accept MasterCard, Visa, cash, traveller's cheques and certified cheques for payment of any duties, etc.

Under the law, no modification to your vehicle or RV, including an emergency repair such as a tire blow-out, is exempt from tariffs. However, in most cases, the agent on duty will waive duties, etc., for the emergency repair. But, take note, a tire blow-out only requires one new tire to accomplish the emergency repair, not three!

If you modify, improve on the condition of, or transform your unit in any way and the modifications are equal to half or more of the value (not buying price, current book value) of your unit, you will be charged import duties on the **entire value** of your RV and/or vehicle. Just like changing pieces of jewellery, any modifications are treated like a new purchase that you are importing.

If your modifications or repairs are less than half the value (make sure you keep receipts and know the value of your unit), then you only pay duties and taxes on the modification or repair. If you have no other purchases, your personal exemption can be applied to the amount.

If you buy accessories to install after arriving back in Canada, these are included in your personal exemption amounts and you only pay duties and taxes if you are over your personal exemption.

Don't try to avoid duties and taxes by not declaring your modifications. We have heard first-hand stories from other Canadian RVers who purchased items south of the border and brought them back into Canada without declaring them. Later, after they sent in warranty and rebate forms to manufacturers, they received a call from federal custom agents and had to pay a severe fine plus duty and applicable taxes.

Don't buy items such as RV appliances and personal goods on a credit card thinking that no one will know.

Two of our friends got caught this way. One couple had enjoyed a $3,000 spending spree in a popular American RV discount store using their credit card as the method of payment. Because they were over their personal exemption amounts, they chose not to declare these items. Several months later, authorities knocked on their door asking if they could prove that duties and taxes were paid on their credit card purchases. Our friends made a costly (and very embarrassing) mistake. The choice was paying the heavy, heavy fines or having their RV seized. They agreed to pay the fines.

Another friend made a major RV appliance purchase in the U.S. and didn't declare it. It, too, was discovered through credit card receipts.

Their deception was discovered after custom agents viewed Canadian credit card receipts from the RV store. Yes, this is legal. The agents then contacted all card holders for proof of paid duties and applicable taxes on all purchases.

Customs Canada is a federal law-enforcement agency under the Revenue Canada umbrella and has a wide-range of constitutionally legal rights to recover lost revenue to our country. The most recent example is of unemployed Canadians who are receiving employment insurance (formerly unemployment insurance) and are supposed to be looking for work. Instead, they have decided to holiday down south. Their custom's declarations were matched with employment records from Human Resources Development Canada and the deception was discovered. Not only are these people subject to a possible jail sentence or a massive fine for obtaining money under fraudulent purposes, they also have to pay back any monies received.

Those RVers who are considering any modifications or plan on updating major items, such as computers or used vehicles, should call Revenue Canada customs for the latest information. This also applies if you're planning to have extensive maintenance completed. Custom import rules are constantly changing, many to the benefit of the consumer because of Free Trade and some duties no longer apply. But, shop around before you buy out-of-country. Many times, with the exchange rate and applicable duties, it is cheaper to buy at home.

Don't take the chance when crossing the border. Become aware of all custom regulations - especially for those concerning repairs and purchases. If in doubt, phone your local custom office. When informed, you won't put yourself into the position where authorities are knocking at your door. In a dispute, it is **your** responsibilities to prove that all duties and applicable taxes have been paid.

Never try to con custom agents - it's not worth the risk of having your RV or personal property confiscated. Make a point of understanding all applicable regulations for re-entering Canada.

Keep all receipts for emergency repairs, maintenance and major purchases accessible for presentation to border officials. If these modifications require payment of duties and taxes, the official will direct you to the office to fill out forms and pay appropriate fees. This is also the procedure when a written declaration for duty-free purchases is requested.

During the winter of 94/95, both Canadian and American RV magazines were inundated with letters relating horror stories of border crossings from RVers. There are always two sides to every story so I won't go into who's right and who's wrong. If you do encounter problems or feel that you were treated unfairly by an inspection agent, address your problems to their superior officer. The chain of command, from bottom to top, is inspector, shift supervisor, port chief or regional manager. You can also state your case in writing to Revenue Canada within 30 days. The complete details are listed in *I Declare*.

Keep in mind that custom officers are legally entitled to examine your luggage (or car or RV). You are responsible for opening, unpacking and re-packing your belongings. You may also be asked to leave your RV during a search. If you don't want only one agent alone in your unit, you may request a second officer to be present. However, this could cause an extensive delay because you may have to wait until two officers are free at the same time.

> *Pick up your personal copy of the I Declare booklet from any Revenue Canada custom's office or call 1-800-461-9999 to order this free booklet.*

Travellers who feel they have been mistreated by U.S. authorities should contact the Ambassador U.S. Embassy, 100 Wellington Street, Ottawa, Ontario K1P 5T1 or, the Director of Immigration and Naturalization, Justice Department, 425 Eye Street, Washington, DC 20536. ∎

Keeping In Touch

Ten or twenty years ago keeping in contact with those at home was no easy task. However, we now live in the computer age and it's more convenient and a less expensive endeavour to stay on top of things. Being aware of what's happening from across the continent is no more complicated than from across the street. Whether on a weekend getaway or on an extended trip, the following methods are only a very few of the ways RVers stay in touch.

Statistics show that Canadians and Americans love their phones and residents of these two countries primarily exist in day-to-day living simply because of extensive telephone use. Phoning from Canada to just about anywhere in the world is relatively simple and inexpensive.

Several years ago automated pay phones with card slots appeared in communities throughout North America (including Mexico) and accept Visa, MasterCard and American Express plus telephone company phone cards as well as coins. When using a card, a voice prompt tells you how to proceed before and after you slide your card through a special slot.

Message Service

The simplest way for RVers to stay in touch is to use a message service. Many camping clubs include voice mail in their benefit packages. Some message services are free for club members.

Other services which carry a small fee allow subscribers to leave and receive unlimited messages plus record a personal welcome message to keep friends and family abreast of your whereabouts. Some telephone companies plus a few private businesses provide inexpensive message services. Many of these limited services are accessible by toll-free numbers from any phone in both Canada and the U.S. and, in some cases you even talk to a real person, not a machine. Check with your phone company and, look for advertisements in international RV magazines for services suited to your needs.

John and I use FMCA's voice mail service and each evening we check the service for messages. This way, we're only 24 hours away from important news and save long-distance calls for necessities. We no longer phone to say where we are and where we're going. At times, thanks to the message service, we even rendezvous with RVing friends who happen to be in the same area we're visiting.

Our toll-free message service number, along with our personal membership number is on our address card. Whether you choose to use a limited service or one of the more advanced programs, using a message service ensures peace-of-mind travel. Thanks to our message service we're never out of touch.

Don't you just hate junk voice mail!

Phone Company Calling Cards

The first step to eliminate frustrations associated with pay phones and the necessity of carrying a pocket full of change is to obtain a phone company calling card. These are free for the asking from your long distance service. If you're a fulltimer and don't have your own home phone, you can ask a friend or relative to share their phone number and card. This card doesn't have to be in your name, however, since you must have access to their telephone code numbers and they will receive a statement of your calls, you do need permission to use their card.

Another option is to use Bell Canada's Special Ledger card. You do not need a home phone number for this card - you do, however, need an address, references and a credit card. Payment is usually arranged by pre-authorized chequing or automatic billing to a credit card. For more information about this service call Bell Canada.

We share the phone number of a relative at our home base. She is also our banking power of attorney. Using her phone card and telephone number reduces costs and takes the hassle out of long distance calling. Telephone statements list the place where the call originated so, when the bill arrives, it's easy to determine our portion. Each month, my sister simply writes a cheque on our account to pay our share of her calling card costs. A minor point of interest, calling card rates can be slightly higher than home phone costs but, the card is not only very convenient, it is less expensive than using coins in a pay phone or calling collect.

U.S. Discount Calling Cards

U.S. discount calling cards are also available to Canadians, if you have an American address. There is no surcharge or hidden fees to use these cards - only a low flat rate fee per minute. Statements can be mailed to your American mail-forwarding address or can be directly deducted from a credit card. The U.S. discount calling card service we use is American Travel Network, under the LDDS plan. Call 1-800-477-9692 for more information. Please note - this particular plan is only cost-effective within the U.S. or from the U.S. to Canada. It is expensive if you use it to call from Canada.

It's also worth your while to note that before placing calls from U.S. pay phones, dial 1-800 CALL ATT to take advantage of AT&T's lower rates.

"Call-Me" Cards

Call-Me cards are a new service from most phone companies. You send them to someone you wish to hear from such as a parent or student at college. Any long distance charges from the person with the card appear on the "giver's" phone statement, much like a collect call but at the same rate charged without operator assistance. A Call-Me card is a simple way for the family to stay in contact. All charges for calls made appear on one phone bill.

"Hello" Cards

These are available from phone companies and variety stores, etc. You purchase these very colourful cards for a set amount, i.e. $20, and the telephone company's computer keeps a running total of time remaining on each card. This is not the most economical method of calling but it does beat carrying heavy coins.

Home Phone Message Retrieval

Telephone companies now sell features for your home phone which makes it possible to collect messages left on your answering machine from any phone. Busy people on the go may feel this is the only way to operate, especially for short-term getaways.

Fax Machines

Although these have been around for many years, John and I retired before fax (facsimile) machines became second nature of doing business. RVers unaware of what these marvellous machines can do are in for a pleasant surprise.

Lawyers' offices, travel agents, stationery stores, postal facilities and many more outlets offer public fax service. We know of no faster way to send important papers across the miles and, in most cases, a signature sent by fax on a document is considered to be legal. The cost of $1 or $2 per page (for receiving or sending) is standard and includes long distance rates. It's extremely inexpensive to send or receive a fax from almost everywhere.

To send a fax, simply dial the fax number (it's like a phone number) of the receiving fax machine and place the page(s) of information in the originating machine. It sends a photocopy of the information to the destination fax. You can send a fax across the world or across the street in a few seconds per page. No additional copies are necessary as the fax machine returns your original papers.

Ham Radios

Several RVers we know have discovered the joys of staying in contact through their ham radios. They call friends and family from where ever they are and compared to long distance phone service, they talk longer and more frequently without paying for the call. Of course, they originally had to buy their equipment and have to pay an annual fee for their licence. Before anyone can be licensed, operators must pass an exam.

In times of natural disasters sometimes the only form of contact is through ham radio operators. To expand your horizons, why not join a ham radio RV chapter of one of the many RV clubs. Sharing such common interests and fellowship can greatly enhance your RV travels.

Cellular Phones

The latest way to stay in touch is with a cellular phone. In the fall of 1993 I was having minor health problems and we decided that a cell phone was necessary. Frequently campground pay phones are located quite a distance from the site locations. We felt if there was an emergency or, one of us had a heart attack, we wanted an accessible phone to call for help. Neither of us wanted to have to choose whether to give CPR or drive to a pay phone.

When travelling in the car we carry the phone with us for emergencies. CAA (Canadian Automobile Association), 911 and OPP (Ontario Provincial Police), as well as applicable services across Canada and the U.S., are all free calls.

> *Free emergency cell phone numbers are posted along the highway and in your cell phone handbook. Though 911 is common throughout North America, not all areas use that emergency designation.*

The following information should help you to understand the benefits of a cell phone. Now that we have learned how to economically use our phone, we'd be extremely lost without it.

When you first obtain a cell phone it's difficult to keep costs in control, partly because usage is very different from your home phone. Although it works like a phone, it's much more expensive than a home phone. The big difference between a regular house-style telephone and a cell phone is that the regular phone transmits sound along telephone wires and cell circuits travel along air waves. Hills, valleys, trees and isolated area can all interfere and interrupt the air waves. Modern technology is slowly reducing these "no use" areas.

While everyone knows that in an emergency the cost doesn't matter, it is very important that for general use you use your cell phone sparingly. Every call that you make or receive is subjected to fees. Charges for each call have a per minute air time cost, even for a local call. Of course, long distance charges increase the cost of the call.

As a result, while using a cell phone is very convenient, it is not very cost efficient. Monthly service charges are also higher than household rates, although, there are a host of rates available ranging from the "emergency only" plan to a full-service package with bonus free air time. You can even get a same number extension phone for your cell. Decide what you want to use your cell phone for and shop around to negotiate the best plan and rate for you.

> *You should buy a 12-volt adaptor for your cell phone. Plug the extension into one of your 12-volt jacks (i.e. VCR) so that the phone runs off your house battery. Don't leave your cell phone turned on and connected to your engine battery because it draws too much power and will run down the battery. If your engine has a built-in computer feeding off the engine battery, it might fail when battery is too low, resulting in costly repair bills.*

Be sure to register your cell home phone number near where you spend the most amount of time because that area becomes your home cell area. Our cell home phone number is listed in Brockville, Ontario, our home base. Our cell covers all of Ontario and Quebec. If we leave this area we can still use our phone, however, we then go to a roaming service. No matter if we are in the U.S. or New Brunswick, as soon as we leave Ontario or Quebec we leave our cell coverage area. John and I try to avoid roam service in the U.S. because each day of cell phone roam usage carries a $3 to $4 fee plus each minute costs another dollar (usage is somewhat cheaper in Canada). There are no free air time bonus hours when roaming out of your cell area.

Cell phones come in a variety of styles and sizes and many have a hands-free voice-activated option to allow you to talk while driving. Phones that plug into a cigarette lighter have a longer range of coverage than battery operated ones. We purchased a 12-volt extension cord which we connect to the

VCR adaptor in our motorhome. It draws amps from our house batteries and works effectively to power our phone. When we're driving, we only plug it into the cigarette lighter as required. An optional phone battery is available but, for us and our limited usage, we don't feel that it's necessary.

More and more people are using cell phones and understand how the phones work. Because John and I didn't know very much about this modern form of communication, we made some costly mistakes in the beginning. To help future owners avoid our pitfalls, I'm sharing some cost saving information you may overlook when you begin to use your phone.

With a cell phone, it is possible to receive calls from anywhere, however, if a person calls you direct two long distance charges are incurred.

> For example - If we are in Toronto and receive a call from Ottawa, the caller pays long distance to Brockville (the location of our cellular home number). We, too, have to pay long distance charges from Toronto to Brockville. This is called Follow-Me roaming.
>
> On the other hand, if the caller from Ottawa dialled a special Toronto roam number before punching in our cell home number (at the dial tone prompt), the caller pays the long distance to the special Toronto phone number and the call now becomes a local call with local air time charges for us.
>
> The double charge also applies if we receive what appears to be a local call. For instance, if we are in Toronto and a campground friend parked next door calls us on our cell phone, she is billed for long distance from Toronto to Brockville (our cell home base) and, then we pay long distance from Brockville to Toronto.
>
> But, if the caller first dials the Toronto roam

number before our cell number, it then becomes
a local call for both of us. A list of roam numbers
is available from the parent cell company.

If you know what area the cell user is in it makes sense for
everyone to use roam numbers when possible. Unless the call is
during a free air time period, there will also be an air time charge
for every minute your phone is in use.

When your statement arrives, check it carefully. Air waves
travel along the water easier than on land. When John and I
travel or camp along the shore of Lake Huron, our calls
frequently connect to a cell network in Michigan. Our statement
shows expensive roaming charges that we never used. Cell tech-
nicians are trying hard to correct this problem for users on both
sides of the border. When there is an error, we simply call our
cell company and receive an immediate refund. Quick and courteous customer service is important to most cellular phone
companies.

Be careful of what you say when using a cell phone. Because
air waves do connect with each other, there can be times when
your conversation is broadcasted to others using a cell phone or,
in our case, to a radio station. Last summer a friend from
Toronto and I were chatting, while John was outside listening to
the radio. After a while he became aware that instead of music,
he was listening to a radio play. Imagine his surprise when he
realized that the "play" was my conversation with my friend.

We love our cell phone and save all chit-chatty calls for after
6:00 p.m. or for weekends (our free air time period). We also ask
family and friends to only call us during those times. Unless
calls are placed or received within our free air time period, we
have to pay for that air time even if it's a local call. This way,
while in Ontario we can justify the convenience of a cell phone
(our home phone) in our motorhome and continue to keep costs
in check. When we leave our cell area and switch to emergency
use only, I really miss this accessory. I always did hate using pay
phones.

Look for a cell company that offers discounts on time and long distance charges. Due to the recent influx of long distance competition, rates continue to drop. Even so, using our cell phone is still one of our major monthly expenses. Though we've described many ways of staying in touch, the most economical and effective way is with a voice mail message service and a telephone calling card. To reduce these costs even more, make calls selectively and choose low rate times such as Sundays. Keeping in touch can be easy and very inexpensive. ■

Accessing Your Money

"That's RV money...
leave it ALONE!"

Automatic Teller Machines

Several years ago when RVers left Canada on vacation, to ensure there was enough money for travel expenses (and emergencies), it was necessary to stash an abundance of cash and travellers cheques in their RV. Modern technology has changed all that.

Today, easy-to-use automatic teller machines (ATM) are in grocery and convenience stores, gas stations, shopping malls and, of course, in almost every bank. They are as popular in small towns and out-of-the-way places as they are in large metropolitan communities.

Since the usage of these machines has become so widespread, it's no longer necessary to bring the contents of your bank account with you on your journey - leave it behind to earn interest.

Banks issue ATM cards free to all customers. When you need

money go to an ATM, insert your card, punch in your PIN (personalized identification number) and pick up your cash. The small transaction fee charged for the convenience of using an ATM is worth the minimal cost. Although the bank limits the daily withdrawal amounts from the machines, it is normally sufficient to cover most expenses.

Our pension cheques are deposited on a monthly basis so we find it easier to ensure cash is available to meet our everyday costs - if we withdraw a lump sum from an ATM shortly after payday.

We then securely file the cash in designated envelopes, each specifically marked to cover various expenses. When I move about with a wallet full of money, I will always find something to spend it on. Nevertheless, I don't feel deprived and I live extremely well when I limit how much I have on-hand. John and I do, however, each carry one credit card for emergencies.

If you punch an incorrect number into an ATM three times, it will either destroy your card or refuse card transaction requests. This happened to us. I had both cards in my wallet and inadvertently punched John's number into the machine when using my card. Unfortunately, that year we were in British Columbia when we discovered why our cards weren't working and had to wait until we returned east of Winnipeg before the bank computer could verify our accounts and issue new client cards.

So remember your number but, for security reasons, never write it down anywhere. Anyone with your number plus your card has full access to cash from your account.

ATMs sometimes fail but, don't despair, there are several ways to obtain money while travelling - besides the most popular method of inserting your card in the ATM. With two forms of identification (usually one of the pieces with your photo) and at least two credit cards, some bank managers will cash a personal cheque.

New banking services surface all the time. In the fall of 1993, Canadian banks introduced banking by phone. Members have free access to the basic service of bank balances and exchange rates. For a low monthly fee, subscribers can move money between accounts, pay bills, obtain statements, apply for loans and much more. Phoning a 24-hour 1-800 number supplied by your bank accesses services. A banking system such as this is a big help to stay on top of business and adds to the convenience of extended travel.

Credit Cards

Credit cards work almost everywhere but, sometimes, the merchant will add a three to eight percent surcharge when payment is by credit card. This is very common especially at U.S. gas stations.

Cash advances on credit cards may be convenient, however, interest begins the day you receive your money, not the day of your statement due date. Some of our friends deposit an automatic monthly payment to their credit cards and several days later make a cash withdrawal. Their accounts show a credit balance before the withdrawal, so they avoid any interest charges on their cash advance.

Some RV clubs and other organizations offer credit cards to their members. However, as a Canadian, if these groups are American based, obtaining their cards becomes difficult. Companies (no matter in which country they are located) do not like giving credit to non-citizens. This, too, goes for clubs or financial institutions offering RV financing. Not too many want the risk of an out-of-country client who can easily take their "collateral" across the border.

Traveller's Cheques

Cashing a personal cheque in exchange for traveller's cheques at any American Express office is another convenient way to obtain cash if you carry an American Express card. These offices will also cash your cheque in Canadian dollars. Each office uses a slightly different exchange rate, so decide if it is beneficial to write your cheque in U.S. dollars or in Canadian funds. If you are out of the country and writing a cheque on a Canadian bank, try to make it payable in Canadian dollars - banks charge up to $10 to convert a cheque written in foreign currency.

There is only one problem with using American Express services - it's easier to find an American Express office in foreign countries than it is in many areas of Canada or the U.S. Holders of the gold card have cheque cashing privileges up to $5,000 in 20 days. Green card members can cash up to $1,000 in the same period. If you accept the currency of the country in cash, there is no fee, however, if you purchase traveller's cheques, they carry a low one-percent service charge.

Bank Accounts

Many Canadian RVers who spend extended time in sun country open an account at a local bank near their winter home. If you maintain an account balance in a neighbourhood bank it is not necessary to wait for a cheque to clear your Canadian bank before you receive your cash.

To receive courteous service and offered benefits, it helps if you introduce yourself to a new bank with a letter of credit from your home bank - especially if you return to the same area and wish to open an account near your favourite destination.

Client/Debit Cards

Debit cards recently entered the Canadian market. When using your bank client card at an ATM, money is directly withdrawn from your bank account for a small transaction fee. When using your client card as a debit card, there is no interest fee because you are not borrowing any money. Debit cards are only effective when money is available in your account. Grocery stores, gas stations, local shops and many hotels and restaurants now accept debit cards for purchases.

These cards have been popular in the U.S. for many years but it is only recently that they are becoming a payment of choice throughout Canada. The main advantage to debit cards is that they limit the amount of cash you must carry. Unfortunately, Canadian bank client cards don't act as debit cards south of the border. (A Canadian debit card is associated with the Interac system.)

As you can see, acquiring money away from home is not too difficult and the available choices of easy access are continuously growing. To protect yourself, leave your cash in your home financial institution to earn interest and, although you can withdraw as often as you wish, don't withdraw more than you need to enjoy your travels. ■

Choosing A Campground

Campgrounds aren't all equal and when you begin RVing, it's difficult to know what features will make your holiday enjoyable or create a disaster.

For John and me, the most important plus in any campground is a level site with good hookups, easy access into the park and sufficient space to manoeuvre our unit. If it's close to highway exits, that's an added bonus.

We also appreciate a well-maintained campground. When park staff trim and remove large tree overhangs, it shows that the owners are aware of the damage that low-hanging branches can do to RVs. Each year, manufacturers are making units taller, longer and wider and parks that provide ample turnaround space for large fifth wheels and motorhomes with car in tow are places we mark on our map as "must return" stopping spots. No matter how pretty a place or how great the amenities, we don't repeat a visit to any place where it's difficult to set up camp.

A steady and correctly wired power source is also important to us. We can cope rather well with either 15 or 30 amp service. But, reverse polarity (when a receptacle is wired so that positive connects with negative), an open ground or power surges are dangerous and damaging to appliances.

Tasty, pure and odour-free water follows close behind a good power source as a significant factor for us. The inconvenience of connecting water filter units, especially on overnight stops, is also a bother. Although you should always keep your water tank at least half-full when camping, (for emergencies), it quickly becomes stale and should be frequently topped up with fresh water.

One other point when dealing with water and electric hookups - we want handy connections. Although some parks have yet to learn what that means, no RVer should need 100 feet of electric cord and five feet of water hose, or vice versa, to attach an RV to hookups.

Over the years, we've found a few parks with easy on/off access to the highway. These parks are made for no-frills overnight camping. At these stopovers, campers set-up within the security of a campground, complete with all necessary - but basic - amenities. Although sites at these campgrounds aren't overly spacious, most are usually full hookup pull-throughs. Showers, too, although hot, may be very basic as well.

Since these no-frills campgrounds are for overnight stops only, there's no need for more elaborate amenities. We love to see these no-frills campgrounds advertised along the highway, especially when payment is usually around $6 to $10 a night and we're en route between destinations.

Other types of low-cost campgrounds charge for only the service used by having a stepping-stone fee schedule. RVers wishing to park within a secure compound pay one low rate. Overnight prices increase depending on what power amperage you select or, if you need sewer or plan to use electric heaters or air conditioners. Unfortunately, there aren't very many no-frills campgrounds available - appreciate it when you find one.

"They aren't from Mars, dear...
they're from Europe."

❖ Highway Truck Stops

Several campers prefer to stop for a nap in rest areas en route to their destination parks - don't do it! In many areas of North America, especially in the U.S., this is becoming a dangerous practice. A safer alternative is to pull into one of the large truck stop chain stations I discussed in the "On The Road" section. Each truck stop is open 24 hours, 365 days a year and, although these are not as plush as five-star campgrounds, they're definitely more secure than highway rest areas.

❖ Good Sam Parks

Many private campgrounds in North America are also members of the Good Sam Park system. Each year, staff members visit and rate each park to determine the quality of washrooms, park amenities and surrounding scenery. A high minimum standard is necessary to qualify as a park member.

The smiling Good Samaritan Angel logo identifies each Good Sam Park where members of the club are entitled to a 10 percent discount on all daily rates paid in cash.

❖ KOA (Kampgrounds Of America)

You'll find these campgrounds everywhere, usually convenient to popular tourist hotspots, in easy access from interstates and major highways. Although every park offers different features, each provides clean restrooms, hot showers, laundry facilities, convenience stores, children's playground, swimming pools and level sites with handy hookups. Many also offer bike paths, hot tubs, saunas, beach access, mini-golf, boat docks and more. Activities such as pancake breakfasts, hayrides or evening movies add to your stay.

At KOA kamps, campers pay for only the services used. Rates begin with a basic fee - dump stations are free but electricity, sewer, cable TV, etc. are extra. Rates are based on two people and there is an additional fee for extra campers, including children, in your unit. KOA franchise owners offer a 10 percent discount fee for those carrying a KOA Value Kard. These are available from any KOA campground or the Billings, Montana head office.

❖ Provincial/State Parks

In Canada, we have many provincial parks scattered throughout the country. The same is true for state parks in the U.S.

Several parks are for day-use only but, others have spacious sites nestled among tranquil scenery. All campers are welcome from backpacking tenters to those in RVs. If you have a large RV, check ahead, although most sites are wide some are short in length. Although many of these parks have no hookups, there's usually a water tap spaced throughout the campground. Washrooms and/or showers are also usually available.

On the other hand, John and I have stayed at several breathtaking provincial and state parks with full hookups as well as spaces for physically challenged RVers, nature centres, paved roadways and paved sites. One park even loaned pre-recorded cassettes explaining the habitat and lifestyle of animals native to the park.

At one time, these parks were less expensive than private parks but they now have a competitive and occasionally higher fee, especially if you are required to purchase a day-use pass in addition to paying a daily camping fee.

In some, seniors who are staying between Monday and Friday receive a discount. However, ask about the senior's discount - in most places it's only applicable to residents of the province or state that you're visiting.

Also check about the no pets rule. Quite a few of these facilities do not allow animals in the campground.

❖ National/Federal Parks

In both Canada and the U.S., day-use or annual fees are required. If there are campgrounds on site, many will offer full hookups plus numerous amenities. Costs can be higher than provincial and public parks.

❖ Bureau of Land Management (BLM)

These parks are located on U.S. government-owned land which isn't being used for other purposes. The BLM (a government agency) provides very basic camping facilities. Rates are inexpensive but, in most cases, there aren't any hookups and very few available amenities.

❖ Municipal Campgrounds

In Canada, John and I discovered that quite a few small towns maintain municipal campgrounds. Payment of the inexpensive camp fee is usually by the honour system.

Some sites have full hookups, others have 15-amp electric only. A water tap will be nearby and most parks have a dump station. Staying at these campgrounds is a superior and friendly way to explore small town Canada.

The above information provides an overview of the various types of campgrounds available. Purchase a North American campground directory from a book store or RV supply store and check with Tourist Bureaus, Welcome Centres and Provincial Tourist offices. Load your RV, find an interesting camping hideaway and get set for the time of your life.

Reading a Campground Directory

If you're using a campground directory there are some things to know about interpreting the descriptions. Remember, although I recommend that you travel with reservations, make sure that you understand the campground's cancellation policy. A number of campgrounds charge a fee if you cancel your reservation - no matter for what reason.

I've listed some terms (in alphabetical order) to help you decipher your campground directory.

- **Back-in** - this means tow vehicles must be detached before backing into a space
- **Boondocking** - another word for dry camping
- **Cable** - a cable TV hookup is available
- **Dollar sign ($)** - means that the hookup or amenity flagged with this symbol costs extra and is not part of the camping fee
- **Dry camping** - no hookups
- **Dump station** - a place to dump your holding tanks
- **Electric, 15, 20, 30 or 50 amps** - lets you know that electric hookups are available and what amperage is used at the site
- **Groceries** - basic supplies are available
- **Ice** - you can buy ice on-site
- **Laundry** - there's at least one machine on-site
- **Pets** - you can bring your four-legged friends. Note: most pets are only allowed if on a leash and, some parks stipulate "small pets only"
- **Playground** - usually indicates that families are welcome
- **Pool** - a swimming pool
- **Private phone** - park owners will share their phone
- **Public phone** - pay phone
- **Pull-through/pull-thru** - these sites allow RVers to set-up without unhitching vehicles
- **Pump-out** - a honey-wagon visits your RV site and pumps out your holding tanks
- **Seasonal** - campers stay put for a whole season, sometimes years without moving their unit
- **Security** - the park provides some kind of patrol and/or security gate
- **Self-registration** - drop money and registration forms into a box, hookup to available facilities and enjoy
- **Sewers** - sewage hookups at the site
- **Showers** - shower facilities are on-site - if there is a ($) next to showers, this means that it will cost you approximately four quarters to run the shower water
- **Swimming** - but no pool listed means that swimming is in a river, lake, pond or even a creek
- **Telephone** - jacks are available
- **TV** - jacks are available

- **Water** - water hookups at the site
- **Water sports** - implies a lake or extra large river for boating, canoeing or water skiing
- **Wooded area** - some sites located by shade trees (don't forget, trees can interfere with the use of TV satellite dishes and low-hanging branches can damage your RV.)

Special Tip For Campers

When you're travelling, even though you carry personal identification, you may not be carrying the address of the campground you're staying at. In the event of an emergency, this information could be crucial.

As soon as John and I check into a campground, we fill out our own self-produced emergency information card that we each carry in our wallet with our driver's licences. In an emergency, rescue personnel know who we are, where we are staying, where our RV is parked and how many pets are on board.

IN CASE OF EMERGENCY

We're _Peggi & John McDonald_

Our RV is parked at _Site 21_

Resort Name _Happy Valley RV Resort_

Phone No. _416-555-5293_

Dates _March 21 - 30_

Pets on board _Our dogs, Susie 2, Maddie & Katie_

During any emergency, please call
Peggi's sister Judy at 604-555-8528

The following is a sample of the card we use. Modify the card to fit your individual circumstance. This security measure is only effective if you complete a new card for each person on board at each check-in. Keep the form with your driver's licence. ■

Membership Campgrounds

"Is this a Members Only Campground?"

Once again John and I feel we hit the jackpot. In our present home resort, the level sites, spacious patios and convenient hookups - including cable TV - complement the excellent recreation facilities, clean showers and a fully-equipped laundry room. An extensive activity calendar of dances, bingo, craft classes, bar-b-ques, pot-lucks, church services and, of course, friendly staff are the icing-on-the-cake on this stopover. This quality park is one of many in the membership campground system.

Although not all membership parks are five-star resorts, many of these campgrounds are nestled among beautiful scenery surrounded by mountains or lakes. Most campgrounds are located within easy access to tourist areas. Whether snuggled in the woods or resting in a secluded valley on the edge of a city, each membership park has its own charm.

Coast to Coast, Resorts Parks International (RPI) and Thousand Trails (TT) are the three main membership park parent organizations. Several smaller groups are in the market but most are affiliated with one of the larger three.

Thousand Trails was the first membership RV park system and now has approximately 75 preserves in its system. They also offer rental accommodations for members travelling without an RV. TT has recently changed its policy and, while overnight use is still free, annual dues vary by the amount of time spent in the park. There is one price for limited preserve use and a higher cost for the opportunity to use the resort year-round.

As the group idea caught on the park system grew. Coast to Coast, now the largest membership park organization, began in 1972 with 13 affiliated parks. In 1973, their independent reciprocal network camping system was started. CCC now has more than 500 camping resorts in its system. Home park members camp free and visiting members pay $6.00 per night. Some campgrounds also include Coast to Coast Resorts (CCR). These resorts combine overnight campsites with on-site RV rentals and cabins. International destinations, discount hotel rates and travel services are a few other bonuses offered to CCC/CCR members.

Resort Parks International includes approximately 385 parks in its group. In addition, RPI also offers inexpensive vacations at many quality condominiums throughout the world. The majority of these parks are affiliated with CCC as well as other groups.

Payment at an RPI park is by one $2.00 U.S. reservation card and $2.00 U.S. cash. RPI also has its own reservation service but, at many parks, you have the choice of reserving or driving up for a site.

The membership park system works by members buying into a home park for site access plus paying a low cost membership into the parent park system. The one-time cost for a home park site ranges from a low $400 to a high of $10,000. The average cost is $3,500. Parent organizations, the area of location and the available facilities all determine park site price. Annual dues can be frozen at less than $280 to $490 and higher.

Memberships may contain a three-time resale clause.

Although, in principle, this option is a good idea, it's rare that anyone reselling their membership will ever recoup the value. In some parks, members can also buy a lower cost one-lifetime membership with no resale value. This is only good for the lifetime of the member. Occasionally resorts may offer a one or two year trial package as well.

On-site resort staff sell memberships in each park, however, in many camping magazines, clearing house advertisements list reduced prices of resale home parks. This is a convenient place to begin searching for pre-owned club affiliation memberships. Annual dues on many resales are under $140.

Depending on each parent system, park members may stay at their home resort free for 14 to 21 day periods. A minimum of a seven day absence must separate each visit. Members can visit other parks in the parent organization twice a year for one to seven days per visit but a minimum of 30 days must separate each of these stopovers.

Frequently, membership parks belong to more than one system - an advantage for members. Some parks may offer one or two sister parks as well. These sister resorts provide an extended stay and home park privileges at a separate location.

The majority of membership campgrounds are in the U.S., however, Canada has its share of CCC and RPI resorts and a couple of Mexican parks have also signed on.

Several smaller groups that have reciprocal benefits with CCC are the Adventure Outdoor Resorts (AOR), President's Club, Thousand Adventures International (TAI), plus others. These associations each have 30 - 50 parks in the U.S.

If you belong to one of the smaller membership groups and the smaller group has also joined one of the larger affiliations and you are told that you must upgrade your membership for another fee - **Don't believe them!** As long as your home park continues to be part of the larger organization, your member benefits are alive and well. There's no need to upgrade with affiliated parks in a reloading program unless it suits your purpose.

There are two main factors to consider before buying into your home park. If a park is close to where you live, you can enjoy the home park facilities on weekends and holidays. But, if you don't want to stay in one area, make sure that you have enough time to travel since you cannot use your park membership at an affiliated resort within a 200-km radius from your home park.

If you buy away from your home area, you can use a variety of affiliated parks close to home. However, you can only visit each resort twice a year for seven days at a time.

Both concepts carry advantages for the buyer but, before purchasing, shop around and consider which organization better serves your camping needs. Ask yourself:
- Do I want to vacation near my home?;
- Have I the time to enjoy extended travel away from home?;
- Do I want to visit a different park for a limited time on each trip?;
- Should I buy close to home and forfeit the use of other affiliated parks in the area?;
- If the home park I choose is one of the higher cost parks, will my usage justify the increased cost of this investment?'
- If I choose a lower cost park away from my home will the number of actual visits to affiliated parks in my area be beneficial?

Don't be coerced into buying from high-pressured sales staff, only you can decide where to purchase. Think about what individual parks offer for the price asked. Remember, when visiting other parks, no matter if a member paid $500 or $9,000 per year for a home park site, everyone should receive equal treatment.

This system works every bit as good as it sounds. Purchasing a park membership can provide many years of enjoyable and inexpensive camping if you follow the program operating procedures.

John and I owned a time-share condo for a while which we were not satisfied with and, because a joint ownership RV park system is very similar, we were hesitant about buying into any club membership. During our beginning years of extensive travel, several rumours about associated problems with these membership parks caused us some concern. But, when we finally took the plunge, within 12 months of becoming a member, we camped more than 150 nights for only $1.00 per night (these days it can cost up to $6.00). Now, we have only compliments about the system and our travelling is much cheaper than in our earlier days.

Originally, we enjoyed the comfort and facilities of many private parks and campgrounds, as well as provincial and state parks. Now we drive a few extra miles to camp in beautiful surroundings at affordable prices. What costs we save in camping we put towards sightseeing and to help offset the increasing price of fuel, maintenance and food.

Special amenities such as cable TV or use of a health spa may cost a few dollars extra. These expensive amenities are not necessary to camping life, therefore, a nominal fee for usage is standard in most resorts.

> To enjoy a worry-free vacation during peak holiday periods and long weekends, I suggest that you travel with park reservations. Resorts, both private and membership parks, are usually full. Without reservations to guarantee your spot, overnighters may find themselves driving around trying to find a campsite.

Last year we joined Campers Club of America. This system works differently because it does not use a home park. Instead, members pay head office a fee (depending on the promotion) up to $1,500 U.S. They also pay dues presently set at $169 U.S. Members can then stay at any of the 250 parks in the system (mostly in the U.S.) for $5 per night. Stopovers can be drive-up only or by reservations through CCA's free reservation service.

Members can stay up to 14 days in one place and return as soon as they have been out of a park as long as their visit - stay for five days and you can return five days later for up to two weeks.

As in all systems, some CCA parks are not five-star but all we ask for is level sites and good hookups. Anything else is a bonus. John and I especially like to travel with reservations so, CCA's reservation service is a big plus to us.

In all parks, guests can choose between reserving a site or driving up for a spot. The central booking system prevents RVers from making more than one reservation without cancelling any of the extras. Be considerate, making excess reservations prevents others (it could be you) from obtaining a site.

During peak season in the southern states, drive-up members (if they can even get in) may only be able to stay three to four days because there is a possibility that the park will be full. However, some parks provide a non-serviced overflow area where members can spend a night. To make sure that you have a site during these busy times, plan to stop early in the day, especially if you prefer to travel without reservations. Expect to spend the occasional night at a private park when the membership parks are full.

Don't be upset if you're refused an empty spot. Not all sites in a park belong to one system. It's possible for a park to appear empty and staff to refuse a campsite because your club's allotted sites are occupied. And, by law, each park must keep open sites for their home members who don't need reservations.

Anyone who runs into problems when checking into a membership resort should call the parent park's head office. The parks are regulated and any reported problems will be investigated. Success of this system is solely dependent on happy campers. ■

"First the bagpipes ... and now this!"

Both seasoned travellers and novice RVers have much to gain from an affiliation in at least one RV club. There are numerous local organizations which provide fellowship and offer assistance to RVers. They all provide advice, RV information, support, offer RV merchandise and so much more. Improving the travelling way of life is the primary goal of these associations.

Editors of club publications, along with volunteers, research problems to find answers to RV-related questions. Technical staff working for various clubs ensure members understand as much of their RVs as possible. Some clubs even act as mediators to solve disputes - frequently financial - between businesses and dissatisfied customers.

Though these organizations are huge, each has hundreds of chapters to meet the needs of every RVer. Belonging to and participating in chapter functions and rallies is the icing-on-the-cake of this lifestyle to many RVers.

Rallies help promote fellowship and provide a venue for informative seminars, new product information, tasty food, camp-fires, sing-a-longs and lasting friendships. Weekend get-togethers are popular and, sometimes, the agenda covers an entire fun-filled week.

Activities such as draw prizes, blind auctions, manufacturer plant tours and visits to local and historical attractions headline each rally schedule. To add a competitive touch to these exciting getaways, rally organizers plan games that include horseshoes, dominoes, mini-golf, card games or golf and dart tournaments. Frequently, chapter activity schedules include something for every age group of attendees.

It doesn't matter how long the event lasts, the benefits of participating in a rally are numerous for an unusually low price. Each club differs and RVers receive excellent value for every chapter dollar spent. For most clubs, there's no restriction on the size and type of your unit, the important thing is that everyone has good, clean and simple fun.

> *U.S. clubs such as FMCA and Good Sam offer excellent club benefits for their members - i.e. RV insurance, content insurance, vehicle financing and hospital/medical insurance plus MasterCard and Visa credit card programs.*
> *Unlike the benefits from a Canadian club such as the Wayfarer Explorer RV Club, U.S. club benefits mentioned above are **not** available for their Canadian members.*

During our early years of RVing, John and I joined five chapters but somehow never managed to make time to attend any rallies. Six years ago, we discovered the joys and low-cost benefits of chapter getaways. We found that RV clubs (and there are many) of all sizes not only welcome new members, they depend on increased numbers for growth and input of new ideas.

Several chapter events are conveniently held in cities or towns close to the Canada/U.S. border to ensure easy access for

Canadians and Americans to join forces. It's a perfect opportunity for participants to become involved, make new friends plus keep busy and informed.

The chapters send out newsletters and bulletins specific to their activities. The magazines include events and changes within the club.

John and I travel extensively in our motorhome and meeting other club chapter members has helped us to understand and adapt to the RV lifestyle. We always feel welcome to join chapter festivities but it is impossible to attend every rally.

Although the frequent chapter rallies are fun, the cream of the rallies - the national conventions - are the most exciting. The majority of RV clubs hold large annual extravaganzas and it'll be worth your while to make a point of attending one of these gala events. Especially if it's like one we attended with more than 6,600 coaches gathered in one spot.

"Hey Tom, are you sure this is the Flower Power Caravan?"

At these club conventions and rallies, dealers along with manufacturers, promote and sell their products at huge on-site RV marketplaces. Browsing through a marketplace is like shopping in a one big toy store for RVs - the variety of products and accessories on display is amazing. You can tour new RVs on display and even purchase the product at rock-bottom prices. We also had the option of attending one or more of the many seminars offered. Each seminar covered a different facet of RVing, from technical tips to learning more about the RV lifestyle.

As I've said, we belong to several club chapters and one year we joined other members for a pre-rally in Lynchburg, Virginia. Five days later, as part of a group of 60 coaches, we caravanned 30 miles to the campus of the Polytechnic Institute in Blacksburg, Virginia for the four-day main event. Travelling in a group added to our pleasure as we could enjoy most aspects of the gigantic rally with friends.

All chapters have a theme. There is at least one out there for everybody such as RVing Singles, Fulltime RVers, Frustrated Maestros (musicians and non-musicians having fun) and many others. Theme chapters bring together a group of people with a common interest.

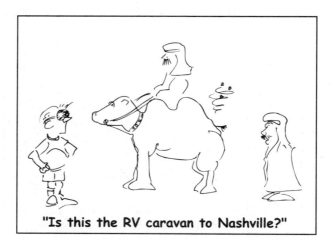

"Is this the RV caravan to Nashville?"

Activities and functions are arranged for every age group - from six to seniors - and include events such as golf, aerobics, roller skating, swimming, tennis, movies, sightseeing tours as well as a variety of entertainment. Daily coffee and donuts and weekly ice cream socials bring everyone together and, at most events, babysitting services are offered to ensure that nobody misses out on the activities.

Fun, fellowship and friends are the three exciting and important reasons why so many of us like the RV lifestyle and each RV trip or chapter rally opens one more door to new adventures. For many of us, time on the road is always too short. Whether full-timing or on a short vacation, RVers who wish to reap the maximum benefits from their days on the road should definitely join an RV club. It truly is a unique experience and a time of guaranteed fun.

There are several clubs and organizations in your area. Ask local RV dealers, nearby campgrounds and RV show exhibitors for the addresses of clubs relating to your interests. ■

Decorating for the Holidays

"Honey, are you expecting your mother?"

If RVing over the holidays, bring your favourite decorations with you. Every year I hear new RVers lamenting over the fact that they didn't bring decorations with them because they thought nobody would decorate when away from home.

To get into the festive spirit, especially at Christmas, pack lightweight holiday trimmings and bring lots, especially lights, to decorate both the inside and outside of your RV. Stick-and-peel window decals also add a nice touch.

At Christmas time, most campgrounds host tree-trimming decorating parties, carol singing, craft sales, breakfasts and so much more. One tradition in the southwest is to place luminaries around each residence or RV site on Christmas Eve. Luminaries are simple candles set in sand inside of paper bags.

Most campgrounds include a Christmas dinner on the activity calendar. Usually park staff provide the turkey, dressing and gravy and campers bring pot-luck dishes to complete the meal.

One campground that we were visiting set up "family" tables

of 12 guests. Each table provided their own food and decorated their table, much like they would at home. At the end of the meal, all left-overs go on a pot-luck table for the rest to sample.

Festivities don't stop with Christmas dinner and carol singing. An extravagant New Year's Eve party brings the season to a close and opens the door to another exciting year.

Don't forget other holidays. Bring Valentine decorations, shamrocks for St. Patrick's Day and bunnies and eggs for Easter. Hallowe'en is another event that is celebrated at RV parks. And, don't forget to pack a costume for one of the many parties you will probably be invited to. One of our chapters annually hosts a traditional Hallowe'en rally complete with costumes, decorations, dances, trick-or-treating and more.

Decorating for holidays is fun, with or without the kids, and it adds another meaning to a popular bumper sticker that states, "We're not seniors, we're only recycled teenagers."

Whether you're a young family or mature RVers, taking part in whatever a resort has to offer adds to the fun. Getting into the spirit helps to make pleasant memories. ■

Protection Plus

Harold...the operator isn't sure
if this qualifies as a
"Road Side" Emergency!

Emergency Road Service (ERS)

There are several protection plans that RVers should never travel without. These plans offer a financial cushion for emergency situations and, even though it would be too costly to purchase every plan on the market, one must have for peace-of-mind travelling is an Emergency Road Service plan.

To date, John and I have logged 11 years of pleasurable, exciting and usually problem-free travel in our motorhome. Occasionally, however, we experience a period when "enough is enough"! October 3rd, 1990 was one of those days.

Due to several impromptu side trips we were three days behind our proposed travel schedule. The opportunity to join friends in Fort Lauderdale as planned came and went - we were simply too late to keep several of our promises. Inevitably, those few times we try to run extremely long days together, our journey is cursed with delays and set backs. Thankfully this frustrating day was not life-threatening nor extremely expensive but it was most exasperating, to say the least.

At 7:30 a.m. we left Pigeon Forge, Tennessee (near Dollywood), heading southeast through the foothills of Tennessee's stately Smokey Mountains towards Interstate 40 - a most impressive journey that took us past breathtaking and picturesque terrain. Unfortunately by noon, we'd only covered four miles. Why, you ask, should it take 4.5 hours to drive four miles? You guessed it - the day's fun had begun!

Our coach is equipped with a "water assist" to heat water en route. (Hot radiator coolant travels by hose to the water heater when the engine is running. Water in the heater becomes hot without lighting the propane burner.) Since this water heating device was already on our motorhome at the time of purchase we never questioned its function nor any maintenance that may be required. (Big mistake!)

While climbing a small hill on a narrow road, our coach's heat gauge suddenly lunged into the danger zone. Simultaneously, smoke billowed from under the sink area. Screaming at John to pull over, my first thought was that we were on fire. With extinguisher in hand, I frantically swung open the kitchen cupboards, although, with some relief, I realized that the smoke was actually steam. A rubber hose had burst near the water heater and hot radiator antifreeze was spewing into every corner of my kitchen. John finally found a safe place to pull over before we did any engine damage.

What a mess! Offensive, oily residue clung to everything. It had saturated our new carpet and at least a dozen clean-up towels. The excess slowly seeped through the floor - thankfully that coach wasn't a basement model. I thought I'd never be able to remove that slippery radiator liquid from everything.

When the inside problem was under control we called our Emergency Road Service (ERS) number. Larry, the tow truck driver, arrived in less than 30 minutes and temporarily repaired the split hose and filled the rad with water. Guided by his tow truck we cautiously limped to a service centre 10 miles back in Gatlinburg.

At noon, we again commenced our journey, our wallets lighter by only a surprisingly low amount of $46 for the radiator hose repairs and additional antifreeze. Unknown to us these setbacks were only the beginning.

Three hours later we decided to end this slow day of creeping through the mountains and stop for the night. Guess what - Nine miles from our selected campground - bang! - this time a tire blew, again not life-threatening but certainly more than we needed.

John unhooked the car a second time that day and he stayed with the coach while I drove five miles to once again call our ERS. This time our understanding road service personnel sent a tire repair truck to our rescue. In 45 minutes we were ready to continue our journey. Events didn't end there - while I was calling the ERS, I misplaced the duplicate car keys. Now with the new tire in place, we spent the next half-hour searching for my keys. They were on the ground by the pay phone, exactly where I dropped them.

Our chosen campground, four miles away, received high rating in the directory that we were using but it was actually little more than a parking place. Not surprising it felt like a five star resort after this horrendous day.

Thankfully we only suffered hours of irritating delays and the monetary cost was, fortunately, rather inexpensive. However, that's not always the case and, although days like this are rare, it's comforting to know that we have our emergency road service to rely on.

ERS plans do work. During our first eight years of RVing, we averaged one to two calls per year on either the car or the coach. Since out-of-pocket costs of only one roadside breakdown will far exceed the price of any road service plan, even if you have to skimp on other things when planning your travel budget, you should purchase this coverage. Annual fees for these valuable RV ERS plans range upwards from $100.

But, before you buy, make sure that your ERS plan offers "no cost assistance with unlimited towing" for a minimal member-ship fee. No-cost means that you do not pay the towing fee up front and only get your money back by sending in a paid receipt to the ERS office. A non-insured tow for an RV is extremely expensive - many hundreds of dollars, in fact. Without an ERS, a towing bill will quickly deplete your cash reserves.

Since your RV is a lot larger than a family car, make sure that the ERS you contract can provide expert RV towing service. An emergency road service plan that can't accommodate the special handling of an RV is a waste of money.

Your plan should also provide coverage for emergency gas (usually about five gallons free), lock-out service, tire changes and jump-starts and be available no matter where you are in Canada or the U.S. Some companies even reimburse costs for emergency service in Mexico. Members are responsible for labour charges and parts provided by maintenance personnel.

Many plans also include the tow or towed vehicles and other family cars.

There should be no restrictions on the number of service calls that you're entitled to nor should there be a maximum distance an RV can be towed to a repair facility.

Before you go searching for an emergency road service, check out what your RV club has to offer. Before purchasing, talk to other RVers and ask what company they would recommend and take a look for advertisements in RV magazines. You'll be amazed at the number of services offered. ■

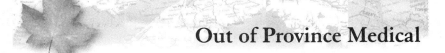

Out of Province Medical

As Canadians, there are only a few restrictions governing our provincial/territory health coverage when travelling. One of the biggest is that we have to maintain a permanent residence in our home province or territory.

All of our provinces and the two territories have individual medical insurance plans, all with different requirements and regulations. The general rule of thumb is that each resident must be present in their home province or territory for at least 183 days. Again, this can differ by a day or two from province to province (some say 181 or 182 days) but, if you don't know for sure, it's better to plan on being home for the longest time period of 183 days.

The residents of Newfoundland have been able to enjoy eight months of travel and still qualify for provincial health benefits. As of this publication date, the process of changing the legislation to reduce the time away is nearing completion and Newfoundlanders will join the rest of us with our "six month plan".

There are certain occasions where your coverage can be extended. This usually only happens when you are away from your province because your Canadian employer is located in a different area. Even then, you must apply to your provincial health ministry for an extension - it may or may not be granted.

The North West Territories requires written notification from anyone who is going to be absent from the territory for longer than three months. This ruling includes Snowbirds, even though the length of time away allowed for coverage is 183 days.

RVers who wish to keep abreast of changes should consider taking out a subscription to either Canada News (1-800-535-6788) or the Sun Times (1-800-253-4323). These two seniors' newspapers report changes in medical coverage and regulations.

There are some Canadians who try to reap the benefits of Canada's generous medical health coverage while working legally in the U.S. (with a green card). Whether you're actually drawing a salary south of the border or not, having a green card in your name will probably end up with your medical coverage being revoked.

Being well-informed and understanding all regulations that concern you is your responsibility. Don't accept word-of-mouth and rumours as fact. If you hear information that is contrary to what you already know, do your research and contact the ministries involved.

Each province and territory has its own cap on how much will be paid for out-of-province/country medical services. All fees are paid in Canadian dollars on a daily, all-inclusive rate. Though all provinces and territories cover emergency hospital, emergency out-patient fees and emergency physician (up to the provincial rate), only New Brunswick, Newfoundland, North West Territories and the Yukon will cover elective health services (at the same rate as emergency services). Manitoba will cover out-patient haemodialysis (up to $220 per treatment).

Because of a reciprocal agreement set up by the federal government, each province or territory honours all health cards - up to the rate set by each province. For example, if your province generally pays up to $100 per day, all-inclusive for a hospital stay and you have to go to a hospital in another province and are billed $250 per day, all-inclusive, you have to pay the difference.

We used to say never cross the border without supplementary health insurance. Now, it's never leave your province without supplementary coverage. This rule applies to all circumstances, even if you're just planning to be gone for a day to do some shopping. If anything happens and you require hospitalization (especially south of the border) a week's stay could put you into bankruptcy.

Even a trip to a doctor while out of province could set you back - maybe not a lot but it will cost you some of your hard-earned dollars. Although all provinces and territories cover emergency physician, it is at individual provincial rates and it is capped. For example: You are away from your home province and visiting a relative in another part of Canada. Unfortunately, you come down with strep throat and have to visit the doctor. This doctor bills your provincial health insurance $100 for your visit. The allowable amount in your province for an emergency physician fee is up to $42 and, for a consultation for strep throat, the province will only reimburse $25 to the doctor you visited. You are responsible for the remainder $75. In some cases, you must pay the amount directly to the attending physician and send the paid receipt to health services to recoup your loss. Again, if the provincial rate for the service rendered is less than what you were charged and paid, then you will only be reimbursed for the amount set by your province and are out of pocket for the rest. Note: if you do have to submit a medical bill for reimbursement to any of the ministries, please do so immediately -- there are time limits.

When buying supplementary medical insurance don't decide what coverage is appropriate on the price of the policy. Read the policy (especially the fine print) and never assume that what is good for your neighbour will be good for you.

Before buying a supplementary insurance, look for policies that cover comprehensive hospital care; out-patient and emergency room services; special duty nursing; prescription drugs in the hospital; and diagnostic services (X-ray, blood work, blood pressure, etc.). You should also find out if your insurance covers ambulance service; air repatriation (to your home, not the closest hospital); transportation of family to bedside; return of remains; plus whatever else you think is necessary.

Also, be aware of the pre-existing condition clause on most policies. If you already have a health problem when you take out insurance, that problem may not be covered and you may have to purchase a top-up policy at an additional expense.

Some RVers purchase policies for the exact number of days they plan to be away while others choose an annual "shuttle service" contract with multi-trip options for 30, 90 or even 180 days. Most seniors' publications have informative write-ups on supplementary insurance - do your research thoroughly before you buy.

Because most out-of-country insurance premiums are calculated on a daily rate, some RVers try to precede their long-term medical coverage with "freebie" insurance offered by credit card companies, etc. This is a service provided by the financial institution to their clients and it allows a limited number of days of free out-of-country health insurance coverage. This service can be a real money saver but, only if you plan to be away for a short time. However, by adding a secondary policy for longer getaways to this "freebie" you could experience problems. If you become ill within the first policy dates (the freebie policy) and the illness extends beyond the limited number of days of free coverage, your secondary (top up) policy may refuse to cover you.

For example: You plan to be out of the country for 100 days. Your medical insurance will cost you $3.00 per day for a total of $300. Your credit card company offers you 22 free days of medical coverage so, to save money, you take the secondary (longer term) policy to start on the 23rd day of your getaway. That way you would only have to pay premiums for 78 days of coverage. Unfortunately, you have a heart attack on the 20th day. Your "freebie" insurance coverage is only good for 22 days so, essentially, you only have two days left for coverage. When you bought your secondary policy (the longer term one), it was purchased under the condition that you were in good health. This policy is not effective until the 23rd day. Because you had the heart attack on the 20th day, the heart attack is now considered a pre-existing condition which could render your secondary policy null and void.

Always read the fine print in any insurance policy and ask questions. In some cases, the credit card company will only allow top-up insurance if you purchase it from a specified insurance company.

Air ambulance service is extremely necessary in any supplementary medical plan. If your policy doesn't include coverage for this service, purchasing a separate policy is a wise move. Yes, some provincial medical plans may pay a minimum amount of 25 percent for air ambulance but this service can cost thousands of dollars and the remainder 75 percent will come out of your pocket.

When looking for an air ambulance policy, check to see if it offers repatriation to your home when you are able to travel and not to just the nearest appropriate medical facility. There is a difference and, personally, if I'm not well, I want to go home and not be stuck in a hospital hundreds of miles from my family.

An emergency flight home can cost many thousands of dollars, depending on how far away you are when disaster strikes. Because emergency medical flights usually require qualified medical assistance and, in many cases, specialized equipment, the costs to you, without insurance, are horrendous.

For example: in 1987, when my sister was injured, the emergency medical flight from Puerto Vallarta, Mexico, to Canada was going to cost $17,000. Thankfully, she didn't have to use it after all. From various points in the U.S., it ran from $10,000, upwards.

> Double check to see if your supplementary medical policy includes air evacuation repatriation to Canada when you are able to travel rather than just to a "more appropriate" facility which could be located anywhere - if not, it may be the time to shop around for another carrier.

Our air ambulance service also includes air transportation of organs (for both recipients and those donating them), vehicle return, family and medical escorts, plus much more. It's reassuring to know that, if ever we need medical treatment, we can recuperate at home near family and friends.

There are other services, check seniors' publications and ask other RVers what service they use but, before you buy a policy, make sure that you are comfortable with the services offered.

> *An effective supplementary medical insurance policy offers more than a low price tag for premiums. Age, factors relating to pre-existing conditions, 24-hour access, length of time you'll be out of province, plus general overall health are some important factors to consider when buying a policy. Read the fine print very carefully and get all promises in writing.*

Before you leave your province or the country to enjoy the world of travelling, become informed of rules and regulations that pertain to you. Don't wait for a situation to happen and then scramble for information and, definitely don't assume that because you enjoy the benefits of being a Canadian, you'll be taken care of - the price is too high. With all the no-cost information available, ignorance is no excuse.

To find out more about your provincial/territory medical coverage contact the office - refer to the directory for the telephone number. ∎

"Oh, great Santa! How do we
explain this to the adjuster?"

The law in Canada states that every vehicle must carry liability insurance. This insurance protects you against claims for bodily injury or property damage. Buy as much liability coverage as you can afford. This is especially important if you're travelling in the U.S. and an accident puts you into a position where you can be sued. Remember, $1,000,000 may sound like quite a bit of money but, that amount translated into American funds, is only $600,000. When considering American court settlements, $600,000 is not a lot.

To protect your pocketbook against costs incurred if your RV is damaged, Collision, Comprehensive or All Perils coverage should also be included on your RV insurance.

Coverage for the contents of your RV is just as important as insurance for the contents of your home. "Built-in" items such as the TV, VCR and microwave are considered part of your RV and are usually covered by your RV insurance policy. However, even though we feel as if our clothes, pots and pans and bar-b-ques, etc., are part of our RV, they are not considered as such.

If you have a homeowner/tenants policy for your home or apartment, there is usually an automatic coverage for contents such as clothes, etc., that are "temporarily removed" from your home. Since this amount of coverage is limited, you should always confirm with your insurance broker/agent exactly what is and isn't covered. There are insurance companies who specialize in RV insurance that automatically provide some contents coverage with the RV policy.

For fulltimers like John and me, it was necessary for us to purchase a "homeowner"-type policy to cover all of our contents and personal liability and this type of insurance can be difficult to find. We obtained this valuable coverage through the Wayfarer RV Plan. Check with the specialists - taking the time to find out where you can buy this coverage is worth it.

When you are buying insurance for the contents of your RV, do an inventory of all of your contents. Either make a list of each item and, if possible, take a coloured photo of every item or, video tape the interior of your RV, emphasizing special articles such as jewellery, camera equipment, etc. In the event of a major loss, you will have a permanent record of all items. Sometimes it's difficult to recall all of your personal contents.

If your lifestyle is such that you intend to keep your RV in storage for part of the year, please, do not try to save money on your RV insurance by purchasing short-term coverage or suspending some of your coverage when your RV is off the road and in storage.

When you suspend a portion of your insurance coverage, such as liability, you run the risk of leaving yourself unprotected . For example - if your RV is in storage (or parked in your driveway), and you have to move your RV a few feet (for any reason) and you accidentally hit the neighbour's fence, you better be prepared to pay for the damage to the fence and your RV. You suspended your insurance for the winter - remember? A definite case of being "penny wise, pound foolish"!

Severe storms (especially in the winter) can destroy storage facilities and, if your RV is tucked away in this "safe" area, it too will suffer. Unless your RV insurance and contents insurance is in effect all year round, then you will be out-of-pocket for any repairs.

If you have paid for storage in a professional facility that company may be responsible for repaying some of the damage. Read the fine print of your storage contract before signing to determine what the company is responsible for and their limit of liability. Be safe, not sorry. Make sure that your investment is protected at all times.

To get the best coverage available for your RV, talk to a broker or agent who specializes in RV insurance - you don't want to insure your expensive investment with someone who doesn't know the difference between a fifth wheel and Class A.

Insurance adjusters assess your property and reimbursement is determined by pre-set criteria from the insuring company . This assessment may be quite different from yours. For example, you may have an RV that, even though it's an older model, it is unique and could serve you for another 10 years or so. The expense of replacing it and the contents could be horrendous. An impartial insurance adjuster will only see an older model vehicle but none of the care and time that you've put into your RV to make it comfortable for your lifestyle. Consequently, the recommended monetary settlement may not even begin to help you recoup the loss. An agent or broker who specializes in RV insurance has more of an understanding what your unit means to you and can go to bat for you to negotiate a higher settlement. ∎

Emergency Nest Egg

In addition to having an ERS plan, every RVer should start an emergency nest egg. Any vehicle breakdown quickly consumes ready cash but, with good pre-trip financial planning, it's easy to be prepared for any costly problems that may arise.

No one plans to use their emergency nest egg funds but it's nice to know it's there if you need it. During our first year of extensive travel, a major mechanical repair made it necessary for us to dig very deep into our emergency money. We went into the garage for a tune-up and ended up paying $3,000 for new brakes, a broken spring, new tires plus many extras before we left. Without our nest egg our RV explorations would have come to an abrupt end.

The incident that started with our broken rad hose (see ERS) was only the beginning of what turned into a long and very expensive winter. We contended with approximately five months of "if it could go wrong - it did". During that unforgettable period, our maintenance expenses rose to $9,500. Believe me, we were very thankful that we had our emergency nest egg in force. By the way, don't panic - a period of problems such as ours that winter only happens occasionally. We previously enjoyed five years of trouble-free RVing, nevertheless, if you are not prepared, traumatic events can destroy all your plans.

Conscientious RV maintenance records keep you up-to-date on when you should have your engine, tires, brakes, appliances (and everything else) checked out. And if, like our so-called tune-up, you find that you need extensive maintenance work or replacement of parts, an emergency fund comes in handy and becomes your most cherished friend. Mechanical set-backs happen to everyone but, with available funds close at hand, they are simply distressing, not disastrous.

If possible, set up your nest egg before you're ready to take to the road. This can be an interest bearing bank account or obtaining a credit card with a high limit. If you choose the credit card, keep the balance at zero and only use it for RV repairs and maintenance.

A well-invested nest egg continues to grow until you need it (hopefully never!). Several financial institutions (especially trust companies) offer many benefits if you deposit over $5,000 in their investment package. When your balance drops below $5,000, all benefits stop. Wise RVers make a concentrated effort to keep their emergency fund accessible and in force.

Shop around and find a banking facility with group benefits favourable to your situation. Developing a nest egg is not mandatory but it is something you should really consider during your planning stage. Emergencies do happen - when least expected. ■

Towing

The new ultra-modern RVs have a number of neat places to pack those items you know you simply can't live without. Motorhomes come with basements, fifth wheels have large storage compartments under the overhang and most cubicles are easily accessible with the help of slide-out drawers. Some of the larger RVs even have all-in-one washer/dryer units and freezers stashed in the under-floor compartments. Most have storage under the beds plus many come with extra slide-out rooms. Every addition contributes to the overall weight.

If your RV isn't equipped with extra places to put additional gear, there are numerous add-on storage cubicles available from RV supply stores. Pods are designed to attach on to the roof of trailers and motorhomes or cling on to the back end of an RV - along with chairs and bikes.

There's only one problem to having all this extra storage - overloaded RVs. Overloading your RV is very dangerous. Too much weight or an improperly balance load decreases handling capabilities and braking efficiency. An overloaded condition can cause cracks in the sidewalls of your tires, resulting in uneven treads. The extra weight also take its toll on brake shoes/pads, the suspension system and the frame.

When the engine and transmission (in both your RV and towing vehicle) works harder to carry an overloaded RV, excessive heat is generated. Engine and transmission failure could result.

Keeping within the weight limits of today's lighter and fuel-efficient RVs is extremely important. RVers who follow a few simple guidelines within load limits will discover that their RV remains in top shape for a longer period of time, providing more reliable service.

To ensure that your RV is carrying a proper load, check the

Gross Vehicle Weight Rating (GVWR) and the Gross Axle Weight Rating (GAWR) of the chassis. The GVWR is what your RV can safely carry with the chassis it is sitting on and the GAWR tells you the amount of weight-carrying capacity each axle can sustain.

Find a scrap yard, RV dealership or feed mill with a truck scale to weigh your RV. Government run truck weighing scales (located on the highway) are fine but, a word of caution, if your load is overweight you will have to off-load before leaving the weigh scale. Unless you have an alternative vehicle to load your extra items into, use these truck weighing stations as a last alternative.

Before driving your RV on to the scale, make sure that the sides of the scale are flat. First weigh the entire coach (record the reading) then locate the centre of gravity and mark it with tape. Move the front of coach off the scale and re-weigh the back end of the unit. Subtract the rear weight from the total weight to get your front axle weight ratio.

To weigh each tire individually, move your RV 50 percent to the right of the scale and to the front of the centre of gravity and record the weight. Back up your RV so that the centre of gravity is off the scale and re-weigh the unit. Repeat this procedure for the left side. Compare the weights to those listed in the manufacturer's specifications to ensure that you are not overloaded. If you are, remove items from inside the RV. If one side of your RV weighs considerably more than the other, redistribute contents more evenly for safer highway travel, improved braking and overall vehicle control.

Always weigh your RV packed the way you will be driving it. This includes water, fuel and propane tanks filled to the usual capacity and all items on board, including the combined weight of passengers. An overloaded unit will cost you plenty in repairs, reduced handling and performance. To protect your unit, try to keep within manufacturer's specifications. These "specs" are posted near an entrance of your RV. ■

If you want to tow a car behind your motorhome, don't go by the Gross Vehicle Weight Rating set by the motorhome manufacturer. The specification you are looking for is the Gross Combined Vehicle Weight (GCVW) determined by the chassis manufacturer (the chassis is what your motorhome is built on). The GCWR is a combination of the motorhome's real weight (not GVWR) and the weight of the towed vehicle. The towed weight allowed is the difference between the manufacturer's chassis weight rating and the GCWR.

Example: The GCWR recommended by the chassis manufacturer is 25,500 pounds. Your motorhome weighs 22,000 pounds (this is just the weight of your motorhome, not the GVWR). The difference between the two means that a car weighing up to 3,500 pounds can be safely towed behind your motorhome. Never exceed the GCWR - you will add stress to the chassis and create dangerous driving and braking conditions.

Once you have figured out how much weight your motorhome can tow, you will have to decide how to tow your car. That depends a lot on what kind of car you have. Most manual shift transmissions can be towed four-wheels down but the majority of cars with automatic transmissions can't be without sustaining damage to the transmission. If your new car isn't rated by the manufacturer for four-wheels down towing, your warranty will be null and void.

Four-Wheels Down

Sometimes called flat towing, towing this way means that all four wheels of the car are on the ground. To use this method a "Y-shaped" tow bar must be attached to your car. This is done by having a professional service mechanic install a base plate to the chassis of your car with the wide end of the "Y" next to your car with the coupler protruding outwards.

If you have a folding tow bar, after hitching and attaching the safety chains, you must drive your motorhome a few feet forward and from side-to-side to lock the tow bar arms in place. Failure to do this simple procedure could result in damage to both your car and tow bar system. You could also lose your car. When using a tow bar, backing up your motorhome with your towed vehicle attached more than a foot or so is impossible.

Only three makes of cars with automatic transmissions have been rated for four-wheels down towing - if equipped with an electronic four-speed tranny. These are new models (95/96) of the Pontiac Sunfire and Chevrolet Cavalier and all model years of the Saturn.

Although, not officially rated, automatics built with a Honda drive-train - Honda and Acura - have been the towed vehicle of choice for many RVers. If you, like so many other RVers, choose to tow a Honda or Acura you are responsible for all mechanical problems.

Another alternative vehicle to look into are those with four-wheel drive. If the vehicle has a built-in manual-lever transfer case, it may be able to be towed four-wheels down when shifted into neutral. If your vehicle has electronic shift-on-the-fly, it is programmed differently and cannot be towed four-wheels down.

Tow Dolly

Using a tow dolly is another way to tow your car behind your motorhome. A tow dolly has two wheels joined by a bar with two short ramps for your car to sit on. When the tow dolly is hooked up to your motorhome, you drive or back (rear-wheel drive) your car on to the ramps. One set of wheels is on the road and the other set is lifted up. Your car must be secured to the dolly with chains or other applicable strapping. Although the tow dolly can carry both manual and automatic cars, those with rear-wheel drive shouldn't be towed this way.

When using a rear-wheel drive, it's difficult to align your tow vehicle to the ramps when backing it on to the dolly. Also, when driving, the front wheels of your car will be constantly rotating backwards resulting in the front end wearing out too quickly and other damage. If you use a tow dolly, you have to find a place to store it when you arrive at your destination campground. Backing up your motorhome with a car on a tow dolly is difficult but not impossible.

Tow Lifts

A tow lift literally lifts the front or rear end of a vehicle off the ground by a special lifting device. Using this system eliminates mileage accumulation and it doesn't matter if your towed car is equipped with an automatic or manual transmission. Unlike using tow bars and dollies, it is relatively easy to back up with this system.

Unfortunately, the tow lift is very expensive, places a heavy tongue weight on the motorhome hitch and hitching is rather elaborate and time-consuming. Tow lifts aren't transferable from one make of vehicle to another.

Safety Chains

Safety chains are a must for all types of towing! When connecting safety chains, always attach them criss-crossed underneath the ball before securing them from the frame of the tow vehicle to the frame of the towed vehicle. Take my word for it, the ball does work loose.

While travelling south to our Mexican hideaway several years ago, we ignored the occasional thud we kept hearing. Eventually John looked back and reacted with a shout. Our car was being towed nosed into the curb-side rear bumper of our motorhome. Our tow ball had worked itself loose when we had executed some extremely sharp turns. Only one hook of the safety chain was all that kept our car connected to our motorhome.

When hitching the two vehicles together, we didn't criss-cross our safety chains beneath the hitch. Criss-crossing under the hitch creates a cradle to support the ball. Fortunately, for safety's sake and our pocketbook, the car never catapulted on to the tow bar when it hit the ground. Now, for peace-of-mind towing we always use our safety chains properly.

Brake Lights

No matter what method you choose, you must equip your towed vehicle with brake and signal lights compatible to your motorhome lights. In some areas, especially BC, having separate brake lights on any towed vehicle over 1,400 kg is a law. These lights can be purchased at most RV stores.

Wiring

Proper lighting on your tow vehicle is just as important as using tow chains. There are several ways to hook up lights from sticking them on with suction cups to wiring into a light fixture from each vehicle.

Our electrician added three-way lights (stop, turn and running lights) similar to the suction cup variety but, attached permanently to our back bumper. Connecting these additional lights was safe and legal.

The wiring was completed by using an electric cord with two male adapters connected to the female receptacles mounted on both vehicles. When connected, on and off controls are in the lead vehicle. There is a new-styled coil electric cable that is more efficient than our straight cable. The coil prevents the cord from dragging on the ground.

Points To Remember

Always double check that the electric cord connecting the lights to the towed vehicle is plugged securely into the sockets.

Because most vehicles being towed four-wheels down require a key in the ignition, make sure that you always carry an extra set of keys for the towed vehicle. It's a real pain to have to break into your own car before you can unhitch it. If stopping for the night, without unhitching your car, make sure that you take the keys out of the car's ignition. If you don't, you'll end up draining the battery.

Before unhooking a towed vehicle always activate the emergency brakes, especially if you're parked on an incline. ■

Towing An RV

"See...this track conversion was a good idea."

Since the original purchase price of a towable RV is usually lower than that of a motorized unit, towables are quite appealing to many buyers. Owners never have to worry about costly transmission and engine repairs. Towables enjoy a low rate of depreciation (excellent for trade-in value) and, because a tow vehicle is required to transport the unit from point A to point B, after unhitching, a separate run-around car is always on hand.

Even though the lower price of a towable seems to fit your pocketbook, before choosing a towable, make sure that your present family car can properly tow your RV. If the RV you fall in love with weighs 4,000 pounds and your existing family car can pull up to a maximum of 2,000 pounds, you will have the additional purchase expense of a new vehicle. (If you buy a fifth wheel and don't already have a heavy-duty pickup truck to install a fifth wheel hitch, then you will definitely have to buy a new vehicle.)

For optimum safety and performance, towables should only

be hitched to tow vehicles that have been built and rated by the manufacturer for that purpose. The amount allowed by the manufacturer, according to frame construction, engine power and transmission strength, is known as the towing capacity.

Along with the towing capacity, another point to consider when determining if your tow vehicle can handle the job of towing an RV is the axle ratio which determines the torque (or pulling power) of a tow vehicle. This designation is always shown as a ratio - i.e. 4.00:1 means that the pinion gear (torque) is rotating four times for every one revolution of the ring gear (or differential which controls the rotation of the vehicle's wheels). Your tow vehicle should have a low axle ratio because, the lower the axle ratio, the better the acceleration capability and pulling power of the car. What is confusing about axle ratios is that the lower the ratio, the higher the number (2.50:1 is a higher axle ratio than 4.00:1).

> *Remember - the higher the number, the lower the axle ratio and, the lower the axle ratio, the better the towing power.*

When choosing a tow vehicle, you also have to keep in mind the Gross Vehicle Weight Rating (maximum amount that can be carried by the chassis of the car) and the Gross Combination Weight Rating (maximum combined loaded weight of both car and trailer).

To determine if your car can tow your trailer, add the Gross Trailer Weight (total weight of your trailer when fully loaded) and the Tongue Weight (the downward force of the hitch ball). The tongue weight is about 10 but no more than 15 percent of the Gross Vehicle Weight Rating. These two, added together, should not exceed the Gross Combination Weight Rating of your tow car.

Other factors that contribute to easier towing are having both your tow vehicle and trailer level and evenly distributing the hitch weight. To see if your hitch weight is evenly distributed you can perform this simple exercise.

Park your car and trailer in a straight line. Make sure the parking area is smooth and flat. Unhitch the car and trailer. Don't move the car and make sure that there isn't any weight of the trailer touching the car. Measure your car from the ground to a predetermined spot on each side of the front bumper and to the middle of the back bumper. Mark all three spots and note the measurements on a piece of paper.

Now, hitch up your car and trailer. When you've done that, remeasure the three spots on your car. Your car will be lower and that's okay. What is important is that your car should be lower by the same amount at all three points. (For example - if the two points on the front bumper have gone down 1/2-inch, then the back bumper should also be lower by 1/2-inch.) If there is a difference then your weight isn't being evenly distributed and your towing performance will be sluggish. To correct this problem, adjust your torsion bars until all spots are equal.

> For an added measure of protection check your tow vehicle and trailer wiring connections and cradle your hitch ball by criss-crossing your safety chains underneath your hitch.

Hitches

Contrary to popular opinion - and, wouldn't it be nice if we could - you can't use just one hitch for any towing situation. Hitches are rated by class and each class is rated by the amount of weight it will pull. Before you buy a hitch for your RV, make sure that you've selected the right one for the Gross Trailer Weight AND Tongue Weight. Hitches are also divided into two categories - weight carrying and weight distributing. A weight distributing hitch is normally used for heavier trailers with a high tongue weight.

Hitches come in four classes - Class I, up to 2,000 pounds; Class II, from 2,000 to 3,500 pounds; Class III, 3,500 to 5,000 pounds and, for heavier trailers, a Class IV that handles from 5,000 to 10,000 pounds.

If you have carefully chosen your tow vehicle to match your trailer (or vice versa) and followed all towing instructions from your dealer, then towing a trailer can be a very pleasant way to enjoy the RV lifestyle. ■

Health & Safety

"It's only you...
I thought it was more raccoons."

Security Tips

Whether you use your RV on occasion or travel extensively, finding your RV broken into destroys carefree travel memories in a hurry. It also adds unwanted and unpleasant thoughts to future vacations.

I've attended several entertaining and informative security rally seminars presented by the Hillsborough County sheriff's office in Tampa, Florida.

We are living in a world of security alarms. However, if you choose not to install one of these sophisticated accessories, a few highlights from various pamphlets that were distributed at the seminars may reduce the risk of a break-in and help protect your home and your RV. I've added several other noteworthy points to emphasize what we learned from RVers we met over the years.

On Vacation

Never discuss your proposed trips in public and don't give information about your vacation to the newspapers, etc. It's safer and more interesting to provide the colourful details on your return.

Several days before you leave, inform the local police that you're leaving. Provide them with a name of a neighbour or relative to contact in case of an emergency. If you belong to a neighbourhood watch, make sure other members know when and for how long you're going to be away.

Instruct the post office to hold your mail and place a stop order on your newspaper subscription. Arrange with a neighbour to pick up any pamphlets and flyers left at your doorway.

Have a reliable person cut and water the grass in the summer or, during winter, to shovel your driveway and sidewalk. It's important that your home looks lived in.

Don't leave valuables in the house. Always put them in a safety deposit box and, on the same line, any extra cash belongs in your bank account.

Any attractive objects that can be observed from the front window should be moved out of sight. In a safe place, keep a list of serial and model numbers of each appliance. Etch some form of ID (such as the first three digits of your Social Insurance number but never your name or address) on to each item. Some police stations even loan electronic markers for etching. (Editor's note: An electric etcher is not expensive and can be picked up at Canadian Tire or hardware stores.)

Repair any broken window panes, plus add locks to doors and windows. Dead bolts are the only effective locks so update, if necessary. Replacing windows on doors with break-resistant glass also deters burglars from gaining access.

Put "toys" such as bicycles, lawn furniture, skis or sleighs out of sight. Left in view (even when locked), these items make easy targets for thieves looking for quick money. This is a good idea even when you're not on vacation.

Hire a house sitter or ask a neighbour to regularly check your home. Give them your approximate itinerary, your vehicle description, licence number plus a phone number of someone to call in an emergency. (Note: a telephone voice message service works well in this situation.)

> In case of a break-in, the neighbour or house sitter should know how to reach you and your insurance agent. Your contact person should also give this information to the investigating police officer when they report a suspected burglary or emergency.

Immediately before you leave your house or RV, unplug or turn off the volume control on your telephone. A continuously ringing phone is a tip off that there's no one home. Better yet, subscribe to a call forwarding service from your phone company and direct your calls to a number where someone will answer them.

Use electrical timers to turn both the inside and outside lights off and on. Have the person checking your house rearrange the time controls to prevent a set "time" pattern from developing.

Unplug all electrical appliances, such as radios, TVs, irons, washers/dryers, etc., to lessen the chance of damage during electrical storms. If the pilot light on a gas appliance must stay ignited, be sure it's in good working order.

Turn off the water at the source to prevent disasters if lines break in the summer or freeze in the winter. (To reduce the risk of pipes freezing in the winter, leave the heat turned on at a very low setting.)

Have a neighbour put one of their garbage cans in your driveway on collection day. Lock the garage and, if it's accessible from the house, secure the door(s) from the inside or add a deadbolt to all entrance ways.

Leave the window shades in normal day-time position and arrange all main floor drapes, shades and curtains so neighbours and police can see what's going on in and around your house. Closed drapes advertise an empty house.

> *Do a security walk around before leaving your home and ensure all doors and windows are secure.*

If you leave a vehicle in your driveway make sure that it's locked. If you're taking the car, ask a neighbour to park one of their cars in your driveway to make your house appear lived in.

Ask the people checking your house to look for more than vandalism. Not all problems occur from intruders or outside sources. Before we began RVing, during a freak weather system one January, a horrendous rain storm preceded freezing temperatures followed by a heavy snow fall. A prolonged thaw in February melted the ice under the snow and the newly developed "lake" worked its way through a roof joint into our fireplace and furnace area. We woke up at 5:00 a.m. to a waterfall flooding two of the four floors in our home. Our immediate solution was to remove the water from the roof as soon as possible. If our home had been unattended for several days, I'd hate to think of the damage we would have come home to.

Installing a security alarm monitored by the police or security agency deters most burglars but it may not be the cheapest way to go. Costs vary according to how elaborate the system. Some programs are basic but others include motion sensors or closed-circuit TV. Installing an alarm may also reduce your insurance premium.

For more hints, look at the travel sections of the newspaper (especially senior's newspapers) for articles on pre-travel security preparation. These publications are also available from most banks and convenience stores.

Security information is available from a number of sources. For instance, the Toronto-based Canadian office of Florida tourism offers these suggestions:

- Don't carry excessive cash - use traveller's cheques and leave jewellery at home;

- Don't lock valuables in your vehicle. If travelling in a strange city and not sure where you're heading, go to a business place such as a restaurant or hotel and ask personnel for directions;

- Park as close to your destination as possible on well-lit streets;

- Drive with your car doors locked, even in the daytime. Always fill your gas tank when it reads half full and have a mechanic check the car before starting your trip.

General Safety

If you have a mechanical problem on the highway, authorities suggest you put your hood up and wait inside the locked vehicle for police to come by. Do not open the window other than a crack for anyone. If someone stops to assist, give them a note and ask them to phone the police or your emergency road service for help. The recognized call for immediate help in any country is to continuously honk your horn three times in quick succession while flashing your headlights.

Officials also warn about the importance of being cautious when using Channel 9 on your CB when problems occur. Some police (including Florida state) no longer monitor this channel. Although REACT volunteers do listen for CB help calls and contact authorities in emergencies, however, be careful - not-so-nice people also monitor CB conversations in search for victims. A cell phone, on the other hand, allows you the freedom and convenience to call your emergency road assistance service.

Vehicle drivers should be wary of where to take a break. One sheriff's seminar I attended suggested to always carry a small amount of cash ($10 to $20) into public rest rooms, especially those at Interstate rest areas during quiet hours. Vagrants may strongly insist on a donation even if you don't feel that generous.

The law enforcers also suggest that you carry just enough cash to pay for gas or restaurant meals. Avoid waving around a wallet stuffed with cash anywhere others can see you.

If you must carry excess cash on the road, wear a money belt. A fanny pack, located in front, allows more freedom than a purse. Limit the amount of cash and the number of credit cards you carry with you. Keep excess cash or extra cards in a secure place. That way, if your purse or wallet disappears, you'll be temporarily inconvenienced, not incapacitated and will be able to continue your trip.

There are several credit card control services available. However, the companies do charge a fee. We prefer to keep a list of credit cards in a secure area of our unit and send a photocopy to our power of attorney for safekeeping. Since we only carry the one card, this personal control is more effective than a service. Always remember that crowded areas, no matter where you are, are a paradise for light-fingered people.

Parking or camping in lonely out-of-the-way places in your RV is extremely unwise and risky, especially in some non-busy rest areas. This applies to any country even if you're travelling with other RV units.

Unoccupied RVs in parking lots also make good targets day or night. It's actually quite simple to enter an RV illegally so don't put yourself in a position to become the next victim.

Some of our friends feel safe camped in hospital parking lots, others choose 24-hour shopping centres as overnight stopping spots. John and I prefer the security and the comforts of a campground.

New RVers may not be aware that there are quite a few free places to camp, all within the security of a campground setting. There are several books listing free or low-cost campgrounds available from RV stores. ■

Securing Your RV

We learned to take safety precautions - the hard way - during the first year of our travels when we became the victims in two separate break-ins six months apart. In the first incident, we made so many mistakes due to our trusting natures that, inadvertently, we probably told the crooks every detail of our plans.

Beginning with a leisurely RV excursion from Ontario to Florida we spent two enjoyable weeks at our timeshare condo. Our RV vacation continued for another month of exploring the sunny south. We planned on flying to Ontario in early January and return to Florida in late March (this was the period when we thought our money well was bottomless) to continue the second phase of our exciting travels.

A great plan, except that I explained our dilemma to too many people as we shopped by phone searching for a secure place to leave our Kruisin' Kastle. Our biggest mistake was that we were proud of our travelling lifestyle and simply wanted to share our experiences with everyone. Eventually we found a place secure enough (we thought) to leave our motorhome.

When the first phase of this vacation was over, we hopped in a taxi, suitcases in hand, from the storage unit to the airport. In an enthusiastic manner we not only telegraphed the fact that we were leaving the RV unoccupied, it was obvious that we wouldn't be back for at least a few days. If the taxi driver was in on the intended robbery plans, then the crooks knew we would be gone for several months.

When we returned in March, big gaping holes stared at us from where the appliances once sat. One thing we can say, the crooks were careful. They removed things without destroying anything. We provided security (blinds were down), tools, lights and a no-rush timetable - great working conditions. They did break one sliding window lock by tapping a screw driver at the corner, providing easy access to come and go as they wished. In our honest and trusting manner, we asked to be robbed.

A difficult lesson to learn but our living education didn't stop there. Our contents insurance coverage for our motorhome was part of our homeowners' policy and, according to our policy we were only covered when we were with our motorhome. Because we left the motorhome "on vacation" while we returned home, our coverage for RV contents was voided. Something good did come out of all this - we discovered that vehicle insurance covered all items permanently attached to the motorhome such as the microwave, CB and stereo. Unfortunately, this didn't include appliances such as the coffee pot and toaster oven plus clothes and other valuables. The price tag of that expensive but effective lesson totalled approximately $3,000.

Six months later we experienced our second intrusion. This time we parked the motorhome directly in front of our time-share condo office in Pompano Beach, Florida. At four o'clock in the afternoon sunshine, some young people entered the locked motorhome through the escape hatch in our shower. This time the loss was minimal because most of our valuables had been moved into our condo. However, I forgot to remove some jewellery, much of it sentimental pieces that belonged to my late mother. We surprised the burglars as they were leaving, but they still managed to get away.

Because these losses occurred before we found an RV contents insurance policy, we were out another $1,000. Small, clear hand prints all over our dusty coach provided excellent training for the fingerprint division of the Florida police department but they never even tried to locate our missing items.

The most secure place to leave your RV is in a storage area in a campground. This even includes the time you spend at home. An RV in the driveway is most convenient but, when you drive it away for a holiday or a weekend getaway, it sends a clear signal to all that there is no one home. (Note: if you are considering parking your RV in your driveway, check your municipal by-laws. Most do not allow vehicles over a certain size to remain in a residential area.)

A friend from London, Ontario, had their house robbed. The keys to a new Class A motorhome hung proudly in their kitchen. The crooks unloaded their house contents into the motorhome and simply drove it off. The abandoned motorhome was found in poor condition five miles away. The fate of this RV might have been different if not parked in the driveway.

Baffling The Burglars

There are many ways to create out-of-sight hideaways to stash your valuables. Unfortunately, since most crooks know more than you ever will about "safe" hiding spots, I can share the ideas with you. However, even if you use an idea, the location of your safe spots should only remain with you. Even if crooks know how you plan on keeping safe, it's hard to steal something quickly when you don't know where it is found.

"Aren't they carrying this security thing a little too far?"

Very common hiding places include stashing small bottles containing valuables packed inside food packages such as cereal or cracker boxes, containers of coffee, sugar or rice. The only problem with this method is that it is so common that any "self-respecting" thief will know about it and will simply dump all of the contents out to locate the hidden goodies.

Attach small bottle lids to the hidden underside of a cupboard, place valuables in bottles and screw on to the secured lids. This method, too, is standard but more time-consuming for a thief who prefers to get in and out with the minimum amount of time.

Install, hide or camouflage a fire-resistant safe. You can also buy an inexpensive (under $30) California safe from K-Mart and other chain department stores. These safes are replicas of brand name cleaning containers or spray cans. They look exactly like the actual product but the bottom removes to access an empty chamber. Place these cans with other cleaning supplies to keep your valuables safely out of sight. Unless you give your burglar ample time in which to rob you, most crooks won't take the time to find out which container is fake.

Attach a storage tray to hold valuables behind the plate of an electric plug-in socket assembly. Place this storage tray and plate into a pre-cut hole in a wall panel. Your valuables are again out of sight and hard to find.

Use the area behind a false panel, under a drawer or some other hard to reach place for a larger secret hide-away.

> *You can share ideas for securing your valuables but never share the location of your makeshift safes or hiding places. Even in idle conversation, the information could unintentionally be passed on to those with questionable intentions.*

Always lock an RV door when leaving your unit. In one campground, a gentleman stepped out for a short visit to a neighbours and, you guessed it, some young kids were just watching for an opportunity. When the kids saw him leave they jumped the fence, entered his unit and quickly found his wallet plus some cash on the night table. He felt secure in his surroundings so he neglected to lock his door.

Cut wooden or metal dowels to fit inside the tracks of sliding windows and doors. The dowels will make it more difficult and even stop intruders from forcing the doors and windows open.

Commercial locking devices, the removable screw-on kind available for patio doors, also work well to secure your RV's sliding windows.

The last and most expensive security measure is to install an alarm system. These range from the less expensive window alarms to elaborate systems with motion detectors. Alarms may be a nuisance but they do provide much needed peace of mind for some people.

The bottom line is that keeping your RV secure begins with being cautious and using common sense. ■

Fire Protection

Unfortunately fires do happen, even in RVs, but most fires are preventable and, with a little conscientious pre-planning and "fire-proofing", you can reduce the risk of this disaster.

Caution and common sense are the two main ingredients in fire prevention. One thing that never ceases to amaze me is the number of people who are so off-handed about their propane supply on board. I can't stress enough the danger of leaving your propane turned on when travelling. RVs move, roads twist and turn, and the motion may cause the copper tubing to crack. A crack allows propane to escape and leaking propane causes a frightful explosion. It's that simple.

> **Adapting specific emergency procedures in your RV could save your life.**

Even if your tubing doesn't crack and propane doesn't leak, every vehicle on the road is at risk for an accident. If your propane is left on when travelling and you are involved in an accident - even a fender bender - you may not have the time (or ability) to turn off your propane. The jarring from an accident could cause propane to spill on to the road putting everybody at risk.

I still can't believe it when I hear of someone trying to light the pilot light on a stove when travelling on the road. Take note - every time that you think it's important to cook a meal so you can eat as soon as you arrive at your destination, think again. You are risking a fire. If you're that hungry, go to McDonald's - and I don't mean our place.

When on the move, the combination of motion and drafts can

extinguish the propane flame, causing gas to leak into your RV without you even being aware of it happening. Even Though propane has an odour, the smell of the gas often dissipates with the air flow, so don't think you can rely on your sense of smell to let you know that you have a propane leak.

Never leave your propane stove (or any stove, for that matter) unattended. If the flame goes out, the gas will continue to seep into the air and a small spark will cause an explosion. Be careful and use common sense when cooking, especially in the confined space of an RV galley. Keep paper towels, curtains and all combustibles away from the stove area.

> *Never, ever travel with your propane tanks turned on. This is a very dangerous practice and could result in an explosion! In the event of an accident, if the propane isn't off at the source and the metal propane connection ruptures, it's too late to remember that you forgot to turn off the propane!*

Even if your fridge only works on propane, drive with your propane turned off. The fridge will stay cool for six to eight hours and your food won't spoil. If you have to occasionally take something out of the fridge when travelling, the interior temperature will only drop a few degrees. During hot weather, turn the fridge up a few degrees the night before leaving.

Always buy an RV unit approved by the Canadian Standards Association (CSA). RVs who have been approved display a seal that is your guarantee that propane, plumbing and electrical components meet rigid safety requirements. If you have any extra electrical wiring done, make sure the work is done by a competent, licensed electrician.

Using electricity incorrectly can also put you at risk for fire. When connecting to campground power, never use a small, yellow/orange 14-gauge, 15-amp extension cord to connect the electric power between the receptacle and your RV. These cords are not heavy enough to support the heat generated by RV appliances, especially air conditioners and heaters. They will catch fire.

All hoses, especially the radiator hose, should be checked on a regular basis. Look for cracking, hardness, extreme softness, swelling and improper routing. Antifreeze (ethylene glycol) won't burn until the water in the solution boils away leaving a volatile concentration. But, the concentration will burst into flames if it drips on to an extremely hot manifold.

When you're travelling in hot weather at high altitudes, your engine could quit due to a vapour lock. Park your RV and try to keep your engine idling. If that's not possible, stop and sit until your engine cools down before trying to start it up again. Never, ever put gasoline in the carburetor with or without the breather in place. The practice of adding gas could easily cause a fire due to engine backfire when you try to start it.

When taking steps to prevent fires, don't forget the tires and brakes. Always check the air pressure in the dual or tandem tires. The friction caused by the low air pressure in these tires can ignite a spark and start burning long before you notice that you have a problem. A dragging brake also causes friction that can set fire to tires or brake fluid.

Keep mirrors, magnifiers and binoculars out of the path of direct sunlight. Remember how easy it was when you were a kid to start a fire because of sun rays reflected through a piece of glass? On the same note, those gorgeous crystal drops that hang in a window to capture the fire of the sun may also burn holes in any fabric in the path of their reflection.

To prepare your family in the event of a fire, hold periodic fire drills. Immediate and calm action will save lives. Don't forget to establish an outside meeting point to count heads and ensure that everyone is safe. If your RV does happen to catch fire, get out immediately. Unlike your home with different rooms, an RV is one big rectangular room and flames won't find anything to stop them from sweeping through.

Valuables should be stored in fire-resistant containers. If your wallet or purse is in fingertip reach and you have time, grab it. If you have to go fetch it, forget it.

> **Fight the fire from a safe distance. Never, ever, under any circumstances, re-enter a burning unit. Items can be replaced, people can't.**

If John and I have a fire emergency when we're travelling, we stop as soon as it's safe without endangering others. Once stopped, John exits by the driver's door, grabs the fire extinguisher mounted beside the door. I grab the dogs, their leashes, my purse and camera (all at ready at the door) and head for the towed car. I always keep a spare set of car keys in my pocket when we're moving. My job is to put the dogs in the car, disconnect it from the RV and move it away to a safe distance. John will do what he can to control the fire with the fire extinguisher from outside of the motorhome. A fire drill while camped or while in a towable will only be slightly different.

You should always keep several fire extinguishers on board, especially one at each exit and in the kitchen. Don't forget to put one in your tow/towed vehicle as well. Familiarize yourself with the escape windows in the bedroom (not all the windows are escape windows).

According to the Canadian Standards Associations, all RVs must be equipped with B and C rated extinguishers. B-rated extinguishers are effective on grease and oil fires while C-rated extinguishers are for electrical fires. All extinguishers must be ULC (Underwriters' Laboratories of Canada) approved. When in doubt, ask your fire department.

Check your gauges regularly. Your local fire-department will be able to tell you if your extinguisher is working properly.

Though Halon-type cylinders have been used in the past, they are destructive to the ozone layer and currently banned in Europe. These units are getting harder to find in Canada and will soon be off the market.

Familiarize yourself with your fire extinguisher before having to use it in an emergency. Always aim your extinguisher at the flames but, only from a safe distance through the door when you are outside of your RV. Be sure to leave the fire area because the fumes from burning material are toxic.

Always store aerosol cans away from all heat sources. An RVing neighbour left a spray can of no-stick cooking oil beside her RV stove and the resulting explosion left a horrendous mess to clean up. Fortunately for everyone, no injuries resulted.

Don't store objects in front of your RV's electrical/fuse boxes, either. This practice restricts quick access to fuses or to wiring that may need attention.

Incorrect portable gas containers are also a fire hazard. Since 1976, Canadian law requires that only approved portable gas containers can be filled at gas pumps. (This rule includes marinas.) No container manufactured before 1973 meets CSA standards.

Approved containers RVers would use are made of metal or plastic ranging from one to five gallons and bearing the ULC (Underwriter Laboratories of Canada) and the CSA seal. All containers must be in good condition with the required gasket and closure in place.

Remember, most fires are preventable but only if you take the necessary steps to stop a fire from happening. ■

Life Saving Detectors

Every RV should have a ULC-approved smoke alarm as well as propane and carbon monoxide detectors. It is important that your fire alarm be sensitive to smoke. Usually before a fire takes hold, it will smoke, the alarm will sound and provide you with an early warning. Smoke is also deadly. Smoke inhalation is the number one killer in a fire.

Unfortunately, in the confined space of an RV, even a hot shower or toaster can trigger these sensitive alarms. Although you may be tempted to disconnect the alarms or remove the batteries, don't. The annoyance is not worth your life if you forget to reconnect. We stop the noise of false alarms by blowing on the smoke detector or by fanning the air around it. If you absolutely can't live with false alarms when showering or cooking, put the batteries in a conspicuous place and replace as soon as you finish.

Propane detectors are also a must for RVs (standard in all RVs built after the fall of 1993). These life-saving devices are installed two feet above the floor - gas is heavier than air and falls. In its natural form, propane is a liquid gas but, when it hits the air, it turns into vapour gas. Both forms are extremely volatile - for instance, turning on a light switch always creates a spark and if there is a build up of gas, even that simple act can ignite an explosion.

Propane does have a smell. Under the law, sulphur has been added to the liquid gas so that the smell of rotten eggs will alert users that gas is leaking. However, air movement can take away this particular smell or, sometimes when we have a cold or allergies, we just can't smell scents properly. A detector protects you against a "faulty" nose by sounding an alarm when the first trace of gas is detected.

If you smell propane, immediately move everyone outside

leaving the door open and turn off the gas at its source. When odour is gone, open all windows and roof vents plus shut off all automatic ignitions. Have a qualified service technician locate the leak and repair the problem before turning the gas on again.

For safety's sake, everybody should have a propane detector. Before we got ours, we had a routine propane check and discovered that we had a leak in our stove top and one outside in the water heater. Because we didn't notice the smell, we had no idea that there was a problem with our propane appliances. Luckily, we are in the habit of always turning our propane off. If we had been driving with it on, something as simple as a cigarette being tossed out a window may have sparked a fire.

Always shut off each pilot light, propane appliance and automatic igniter when you are filling your RV's gas tank. When refilling the propane cylinder, shut off the cylinder's supply and only fill the propane tank to a maximum of 80 percent. Any excess should be bled off through the pressure release valve.

Never allow anyone to tamper with or seal this release valve. If the pressure in your tank changes because of temperature fluctuations, the release valve regulates the tank or cylinder pressure. In a properly filled tank there should be no reason to release gas, even if you have travelled from the cold north to the sunny south.

There are different types of detectors on the market. Some only sound an alarm when gas or liquid is present while others have a solenoid valve to shut off the flow of gas. Most units operate on the 12-volt system.

Hand-held propane detectors, operated by rechargeable or standard D-cell batteries, are also available. Though costly, these small devices are very handy in detecting small leaks throughout the system.

Carbon monoxide (CO) gas is an insidious killer that lulls you into a sleep from which you never wake. It's odourless, colourless, tasteless - totally invisible. It collects in enclosed places and, unless you have a detector, you don't know that it's there. Don't be its next victim.

If you are awake and are in an enclosed RV, car or, even a house, and start to feel headachy (even slightly), any drowsiness, sick to your stomach, weak, start to vomit or experience heart palpitations, immediately open a window and get out into the fresh air! Because carbon monoxide poisoning robs you of common sense and causes disorientation, you may not even be aware that you are poisoned. A coma, heart attack and death usually results. Because the symptoms mimic the flu, motion sickness, food poisoning, etc., you may be tempted to just pass off the feeling and curl up in bed. Don't.

Carbon monoxide can take a while to build up and, because it is the same weight as air, it mixes easily and freely moves around. A CO detector should be installed four feet off the floor and should be placed in your main living area as well as your sleeping area.

> Some carbon monoxide and propane detectors are so sensitive that they will react to hair spray, alcohol, exhaust fumes, paint cleaners, sewer gases, glue and, even the chemical treatment on new carpeting. Although it can become tiresome, never assume that your alarm is being triggered by something harmless - engage in evacuation procedures until you can safely check it out.

Furnace fumes, exhaust fumes from a generator and vapours from other vehicles all contribute to the accumulation of this gas. You're asking for trouble if you keep your generator running while sleeping. Parking too close to idling vehicles in rest areas or camped next to an RV running a generator can also put you at risk for carbon monoxide poisoning.

If you can't avoid the later two situations, keep all doors and windows closed and coach exhaust vents on to minimize the risk. Spend the money and cut the risk - install a carbon monoxide (CO) detector now.

How To Avoid CO Poisoning

Before setting out on a trip check your exhaust system and generator to make sure all are running properly. The tip of your exhaust pipe should extend beyond the outer wall of your RV. If there is damage, replace the exhaust pipe. Do not use flexible piping as it can leak. All propane appliances should have bright burning flames. If the flame is red or yellow there is insufficient combustion which creates a high level of CO.

Don't place objects directly in front of the furnace vents and inspect the walls and floors of your RV for openings that could allow fumes to enter. When you are travelling, always keep your rear windows and vents closed. While the RV is moving, a low pressure is created drawing gas fumes into your RV. When travelling in heavy traffic or going through a tunnel, the exhaust fumes of other vehicles may be seeping into your RV. If you or your passengers start to feel woozy or exhibit the other symptoms mentioned above, immediately pull over and get out into the fresh air. If symptoms remain present or worsen, seek medical help.

> *When using your generator, close all windows above or near this power source.*

Don't park so that your exhaust faces towards a wall or fence - the exhaust will bounce back the fumes to your coach. Never run the engine or generator in an enclosed area such as a service centre or garage.

When using the stove or oven, turn on the fan to remove gases. Never use the stove to heat the unit - carbon monoxide is released from the propane burners.

Don't bet your life on "just this time it'll be okay". Carbon monoxide kills. ■

First Aid

One perfect, sunny February afternoon in Texas, while swimming with new-found RVing friends, a wasp landed on my back and stung me, leaving me in excruciating pain. That winter my blood pressure was somewhat erratic and this situation didn't help.

When I felt my heart racing and the beginning of palpitations, I was close to panic. Someone suggested I put a paste of baking soda on the sting to draw out the venom. Since I had no known allergies to insect stings, my neighbour drove me home instead of to a hospital.

As we travel, many RVers pass on hints for situations such as this, however, I tend to forget them as fast as I hear them. As the immediate shock subsided, my blood pressure decreased but, my back still ached. I reached for our medical reference book to find a simple way to relieve my discomfort. We carry The Doctors Book Of Home Remedies, published by Preventive Magazine Health Books, Emmanaus, PA 18098, just for this type of situation.

This book is filled with hints that work well when dealing with minor medical problems. Although it's a great book to have on hand, fortunately, we haven't had to use it that often.

Our book suggested that the way to lessen the discomfort of stings from jelly-fish, bees and wasps was to put a paste of baking soda or sand on the sting and after several minutes, take a plastic card or a flat table knife and scrape the top of the bite to remove the stinger.

Amazing, but it worked. Almost immediately after John scraped the sting area, all pain went away. I guess he removed the last traces of the stinger.

Whether you choose this manual or some other one, RVers should carry some form of medical reference book, plus a well-stocked first-aid kit. Many hints and suggestions on how to handle minor medical situations are especially beneficial when doctors and medical clinics are a distance away from your campsite.

Carrying a completely stocked first-aid kit is extremely important, especially when you're parked in an out-of-way area. Your first-aid kit should be keep in an easily accessible and, ideally, you should have a large kit in your RV and a smaller one for your tow car.

A properly stocked kit should contain a basic first-aid manual, scissors, tweezers, bandages (strip and butterfly), gauze (both strip and pre-cut packaged dressings), adhesive tape, no-stick burn dressing, pressure pads, slings and an assortment of different size safety pins. Medications should include an antiseptic cream for minor cuts and wounds, sunburn ointment and your family's analgesic for pain. A personalized supply of antihistamine (capsules and/or Benadryl) should be included in case of a reaction from a sting. Anyone who suffers from anaphylactic shock should always carry their epinephrine (Epi-pen, ephedrine) kit with them. Special note: Never share over-the-counter or your prescription medications with anyone. Your prescription may be poison to them.

> *If you are allergic to stings be careful when travelling south. Bites from fire ants can trigger a very severe anaphylactic reaction.*

Though no one anticipates an emergency, it's comforting to have a basic kit. Besides knowing to scrape a sting and to never pull the stinger out with tweezers, there are a few other basic first-aid points to keep in mind.

If victim has fallen (or in a car accident) and it is safe to leave them where they are, do not move the person - there may be spinal injuries. Call an ambulance and let trained paramedics take over.

Never, ever administer medication to an accident victim. You have no way of knowing if they have allergies and your so-called "helpful" treatment may kill them.

Anyone who has suffered a trauma is subject to shock. Keep patient warm and watch carefully. Shock victims can become confused and often start wandering.

To staunch bleeding, apply pressure directly to the wound. If the pad becomes soaked, apply another one right over it - do not remove the old one. If bleeding persists, seek medical help.

Nose bleeds, though fairly common, can become severe. In the case of a nose bleed, never tilt the head back. Tilt the head forward and lightly pinch the bridge of the nose - a couple of seconds at a time. Apply a cold compress to the back of the neck. If the nose bleed doesn't stop or the flow is heavier or there is clotting seek medical help.

Burns should not be treated with grease. Do not rub butter on a burn. Instead, cool the burn with cold (not ice) water. Use a sterile burn pad and do not cover the affected area with a tight bandage.

Apply wet dressings to scrapes, road burns or rope burns. The moisture in the dressing cools the burn.

Learn the basics of blood pressure monitoring, CPR (Cardiac Pulmonary Resuscitation) and artificial resuscitation. Knowing how to perform CPR could, one day, save the life of a loved one.

St. John's Ambulance, some high schools and community colleges offer lifesaving courses. Take the time to learn the techniques or to keep your training current.

Snake Bites

As children, many of us were Cubs, Scouts, Brownies or Girl Guides and we learned to always "be prepared". RVers should follow this same practice. Before you begin tramping through the wilds or into an unknown area, visit the local library, stop at local tourist welcome centres, talk to RVers camped nearby or have a discussion with staff members at provincial, state and national parks. Learn what you can about the habits and lifestyles of local wildlife. When you know what to expect, you'll see more because you'll be alert to small tell-tale signs that signify what creatures live beyond the trail.

One procedure all travellers should become familiar with is what to do about a snakebite. Since most of us don't know the difference between a poisonous and non-poisonous snake, if you get bitten wash the bite with soap and water. Keep the victim quiet and still and immediately call an ambulance or get to a hospital.

If possible, kill or capture the snake (without risking a second bite) to bring along for identification. If you can't kill or catch the snake, try to remember what it looked like.

Don't think about playing hero and cut into the snakebite and sucking out the poison. This practice is dangerous to both the victim and the "hero". Doing this or applying an ice-pack is extremely traumatic to the body's natural defence and it raises the chance of infection.

"Ernie, Bert & Nick will keep the RVers in their motorhome till we've finished dinner."

Do not apply a tourniquet. Tourniquets can cause far more damage than the snakebite. Improperly applied, they can cause loss of blood flow and possibly gangrene, resulting in required amputation of the limb. Remember, for the best help, immediately transport the victim to a medical facility or call an ambulance.

Feeding Folly

Every year we hear of people attacked or mauled by bears, wolves and other wild animals. In real life, wild animals are not pets so, forget Yogi the Bear and Bambi, do not approach any animal that does not belong to you. Do not stand too close to any animal or reptile - this could violate their territorial rights, especially if the young are present - and you will be attacked.

In the same vein, do not feed wild animals. They will become dependent on hand-outs and, when food supplies stop, they will become aggressive and terrorize a campsite to get at the "free" goodies.

When you are out of your element and in theirs, respect the fact that you are in their home - and treat it as such. Don't create a situation that could endanger your life. ■

Ability Plus

As John and I travel the countryside we meet many warm and friendly people and, although each person is special, occasionally we meet someone who is simply unforgettable.

Such was the case when a 40-foot motorhome settled into the site next to ours in a Louisiana campground. Nothing appeared unusual until the driver turned off the engine and climbed from his motorhome to sit in his wheelchair.

This American RVer lost his legs in Vietnam and he and his wife decided that instead of sitting around and feeling sorry for themselves, they would get on with the art of living. And, part of their new life was travelling around in their RV with a car in tow.

It sounded almost unbelievable when he told us how inexpensive and easy it was to modify their RV. Immediately after purchasing their motorhome, the couple phoned Gresham Driving Aids, Inc., to order modified operating equipment. Three days later a hand-control system arrived and, shortly after, their coach was ready and waiting for a test ride.

Using only a hand lever, our new friend has full control of his vehicle brake and his accelerator - each operates separately. He can also use both pedals at the same time when necessary (for parking, going up a hill from a stop, etc.).

Gresham's driving modifications fit each vehicle by year, make and model. Most conversion equipment is not transferable to alternate vehicles without additional parts supplied by the manufacturer.

Mr. Gresham, himself a quadriplegic, worked together with his family to design and develop each driving aid. Several of Gresham conversions assist disabled drivers to operate their vehicle. Other modifications allow people who can't walk to travel away from their homes in vans equipped for wheelchairs.

Since our first encounter with physically challenged RVers,

we've talked to several others who have taken to the road against all odds. One fall, while touring the southwest, John and I met another physically challenged RVer and his wife who were also experiencing the joys of RV living. When this RVer lost use of his legs, he had a new RV sitting in their driveway. Instead of sitting back and letting the world go by, this adventurous couple searched to find a way to accommodate their new lifestyle. They had places to go and things to see and, with conversions, his medical problems were only an inconvenience, not an obstacle.

At one of our national conventions, John and I talked to various members from a chapter called the Achievers made up of members with disabilities and their partners. The members of this chapter routinely deal with a variety of medical problems, however, nothing deters them from participating in the many pleasures associated with life on the road. To become a member of the Achievers chapter, call FMCA for more information.

We met another RVer and his wife (also members of the Achievers) from Canada who turned their disabilities into abilities. At times their RV fantasy followed a rough and rocky road, depending on their health of the moment.

During the mid-80s, he was diagnosed with post-polio syndrome, an ailment that attacks an adult who suffered from polio as a child. In time, this latent polio disease restricts breathing plus slowly decreases most leg muscle control. The periodic assistance of a respirator sometimes helped his breathing.

His wife's health, too, was less than perfect. She has MS, a disabling illness that causes abnormal hardening of body tissue. This couple loves RVing but prefer to dry camp so that they can participate first hand in all aspects of nature. Because of the vast amount of equipment necessary to cope with their everyday living, their motorhome doubles as a car. It's easier for them than pulling a separate vehicle.

After our new acquaintance purchased a mobility scooter for herself, these two wanderers explored each destination - she simply towed her husband's wheelchair behind her "freedom machine". Mobility scooters provide another dimension of freedom, especially the new compact models that fold to fit into the trunk of a car or RV storage pods. A series of 27 on board batteries plus a heavy-duty generator to power the scooter and required respirators was installed in their unit.

Her mother also liked exploring RV hideaways and she, too, didn't let her heart and asthma problems interfere. By simply packing her breathing machine, she was ready to relish each of her experiences.

RVers with disabilities don't waste time thinking about what isn't available to them, nor do they allow anything to disrupt their RV travels - they just do it their way.

Each year, more and more tourist attractions, national monuments, private campgrounds plus provincial and state parks add wheelchair accessibility to their facilities.

In Canada and the U.S., there are many companies that offer conversion service for RVers with disabilities. As well as providing hand-controls for driving, these companies can install hydraulic lifts, widen doorways (for wheelchair access) and do a number of adjustments to make an RV handicap accessible.

> *Before using an American conversion service, check with Canada Customs for duty information.*

Campgrounds, too, are making facilities available to people who are physically challenged. Many are upgrading washrooms and showers to "user friendly" facilities. They're also installing ramps into buildings and creating sites that offer easy access for the physically challenged. When choosing a campsite, look for the universal handicap symbol.

All the RVers with disabilities who we've met on the course of our travels have found a way to turn their fantasy lifestyle into a reality and each one offered the same message...

"Life is too precious to waste any of it. Sitting around while opportunities pass you by is not

living, it's only existing. Don't wait for some-
day...do what you want to now while you're
able. If following your dream means travelling
in an RV, find a way and just do it!"

Appreciate North America's natural beauty at your convenience - turn your disability into an ability. Follow your heart
and, with a little luck and a lot of determination, we may see you
in one of North America's interesting campgrounds. ■

Fulltiming

"Honey...Do you think maybe
we should move on?"

Budgeting for the Good Life

"I say...you must be rich to enjoy this RV lifestyle...ehh?"

A year or so ago, I received a letter in response to one of my columns suggesting that John and I must be rich to travel the way we do. I can assure the writer (and anyone else who thinks the same) that not too many RVers (including ourselves) on the road today are what could be described as rich, or even remotely wealthy. Most of us have simply discovered how to live comfortably within whatever retirement income we receive.

Our logo, "Goodbye Tension, Hello Pension", says it all. Once we learned that the "money well" had a bottom to it and each month there's only a fixed amount to fill it up again, we adjusted our lifestyle accordingly and living on a pension became an acceptable way of life.

We also realize that many RVers can only use their RVs for weekend excursions and during vacations. The following money saving tips apply equally to all RVers. Just weed out anything not applicable to your lifestyle.

This information guideline is based on two people enjoying

an extended trip. When you draw up your budget consider your personal lifestyle, hobbies, interests and the number of people travelling in your unit - this alters the living expenses. Every situation is unique and, although some RVers exist on a monetary output of $750 per month, others need $3,500 or more. The average Canadian RVer finds a happy medium between those two figures.

Don't assume that, because the couple in the unit next to you has a very elaborate Class A motorhome, they must be rolling in dough to be able to afford that and a house somewhere else. Many retired RVers liquidate all material assets, including the house, before buying an RV. Instead of an extra luxury, their RV may be their only home.

When John and I retired, we sold our house and we eliminated $13,000 of annual expenses. Over the years we have learned to fine-tune our living expenditures even more.

For us, many costs such as property taxes, home insurance, the second car, cable TV, home phone, heating, water and so on became obsolete. Dry cleaning expenses were also history (for the most part) since casual and washable clothing is much better for the relaxed lifestyle of RV travelling. One amount that remains fairly constant is the cost of food - after all, no matter where you live you have to eat. Our biggest change was cutting back on the times we ate out - dining in expensive restaurants does not go well with a fixed pension income.

If you have RV loan payments, include them in your budget just as you would a mortgage on a house and, if you have always been an avid golfer or have any other costly hobbies, add those in as well. Quite a few RVers choose to forego those type of hobbies and substitute them for free ones such as hiking, fishing, bird watching and other nature related alternatives. A number of campgrounds also help RVers stretch their budget with free activities such as movie nights, card games, bingos, craft classes, billiard tables and shuffleboard.

There are two expenses that are not possible to eliminate - gas and camping fees. Nevertheless, with a little pre-planning, you can reduce these costs to a livable range.

For instance, John and I budget $500 monthly for camping/fuel costs. Because we don't pay high camping fees when travelling and we don't pay for RV fuel when stopping for extended periods, the two costs balance each other making this expense an either/or situation.

We joined several membership park systems in 1990, five years after we began RVing. Now while travelling between northern and southern regions, we camp at member campgrounds for $6.00 - $9.00 per night. By staying in the membership park system, our camping fees are low so the allotted $500 per month is used mainly on gas.

In contrast, because we stay for a longer time at destination parks - we reserve a minimum of one month (three months during the busy winter season) - our cost is much lower than the daily (per night) rate.

RVers on vacation may not be able to enjoy a leisurely pace but, all RVers should try to tour a bit of each area during a stopover. Cooking and eating your meals in the comfort of your home-on-wheels saves "restaurant" money for more interesting pursuits.

During our first years of extensive travelling, the exchange rate was acceptable and we didn't bother with excessive budgeting. So every dollar we spent bought a dollar's worth of goods. However, after spending seven years on the road, with no pay increases, we learned how to stretch each dollar so we could continue our lifestyle in comfort. It was a challenge at times but mostly fun to see how many corners we could cut and still enjoy ourselves.

Every RVer has different needs. On the next page is a sample of our on-the-road living expenses. Although at times we travel on a tight budget (and sometimes have to dig into our reserve), we try not to travel on a tight schedule.

This is only a guideline for budgeting expenses - add and subtract your own costs. Everything has been listed in Canadian dollars. Any conversions made to accommodate the rate of exchange between Canadian and U.S. funds was calculated at 40 percent.

EXPENSE BUDGET

Monthly Living Expenses

Camping/gas	500
Food/groceries/entertainment	600
Phone - long distance	100
Clothes/miscellaneous	100
Total	**$ 1,300**

($1,300 x 12 months = $15,600 annual)

Fixed Monthly Expenses

RV/car payments	-----
Insurance (car, RV, RV content)	175
Storage unit	45
Life insurance	65
Cell phone service (May-Oct)	50
Mail forwarding & postage	20
Banking fees (telephone service)	9
Total	**$ 364**

($364 X 12 months = $4,368 annual)

Annual Club Expenses

Wayfarer Explorer RV Club	25
FMCA	35
Good Sam	28
Camping World/President's Club	30

Five chapters/FMCA		70
Membership parks		
CCC		91
RPI		70
Camper's Club Annual Dues		209
Membership park maintenance fees		265
Air Force Association		15
Atlantic Chief and PO's Association		20
Total	$	**858**

Annual Living Expenses

Medical insurance (variable approx.)	1,000
Tax preparation (2)	100
Credit card fees (3)	140
Cell phone licence	60
Dogs (3) shots/medical	200
Vehicle licence (2)	132
Driver's licence (2) (per year)	20
Banking power of attorney and	
Canadian mail forwarding assistance	150
Vehicle maintenance budget*	3,000
Emergency road service	100
Air ambulance (2)	235
Total	**$ 5,197**

* We keep a modest reserve fund for unplanned surprises. Our vehicle maintenance budget varies but, we always maintain an emergency fund for "just in case". It's better to be prepared than to be sorry.

Use the above ideas to design your personalized budget. Note: Club membership dues are based on the fact that we are members. RV clubs usually charge a very low initiation fee (about $10) when you first sign up.

> Contrary to popular belief, although stores in the U.S. have an extensive selection, many food prices in the U.S. are generally equal to Canadian prices dollar for dollar. Including the rate of exchange in the overall price, groceries are not a bargain.

Our budget is set for our lifestyle, not yours. Keep in mind that if your RV is less than 38 feet, your insurance rates may be lower. Using the club affiliations, as we do, or the cell phone or some of our other expenses may also be unnecessary. On the other hand, if you play expensive sports such as golf or tennis, or like to eat out, take in a stage show or go on shopping sprees, your costs may be higher than ours. All travel styles differ.

Note: If I make any crafts, the costs come from our miscellaneous spending and, if I sell them at park craft sales, any money earned is set aside to buy more supplies.

Credit Applications

Most people don't have the cash to plunk down to pay for an RV. Even if you've sold your house, you may want to invest a majority of the amount received. Unfortunately, lending institutions have traditionally frowned on financing "mobile" purchases, especially if that purchase is going to be your home and can be moved at will. Essentially, the collateral can literally drive away and it's difficult to recoup in the event of default.

Another reason why it's difficult to obtain financing is because of certain questions you must answer on any credit application pertaining to residence status.

Even though we keep a room in a relative's house, we do not pay rent. So, every time we were faced with answering "Do you own your home?" or "Do you rent (an apartment or room)?" and "How much do you pay?", we were thrown into a tail-spin because we didn't know how to answer. We simply don't fit the mould of a house with a white picket fence that so many non-RVers find necessary.

Our RV is our home (to us, not a bank) and our room is also part of our residence but, because we don't pay rent, the bank doesn't consider it such. We have always avoided approaching any financial institutions for credit because of these questions. When we bought our motorhome, we felt as if we had no choice but to use dealer financing which, although appreciated, was slightly more costly than a plan through a bank. Even though this amount wasn't that much extra, when you're on a pension, every penny counts.

At the Motorhome and Trailer Show (International Centre, Malton, Ontario), we talked to representatives from the Bank of Montreal who were offering a very low interest loan for show buyers. They didn't know who we were so we could be very honest about our fulltime status. The reps listened and, after I said that we didn't know how to respond to the questions and qualify for a loan, they informed us that the additional part to the above-stated questions was - "Do you live with parents?", or "Other?".

Finally, a category we fall under - we are definitely "other"!

According to the definition of the other category, we do own a home - with wheels and, we do pay rent - to campgrounds. What a relief to finally come out in the open and, once again, qualify for a mortgage or loan.

Canadian Pensions

All Canadian senior citizens receive a pension if they qualify for a residency claim. Pensioners with up to twenty years residency receive a partial pension but, with forty years of living in Canada, seniors receive the maximum amount of Old Age Security (OAS) available.

We have a friend who lives in the U.S. He only worked seven years in Canada but, at age 65 received an OAS pension of $18 per month. Hardly a fortune but he earned it. Those qualifying can collect this pension without penalties at the age of 65 but, this pension may be taxable as income received in your country of residence.

Any senior who, after receiving OAS, is still below the poverty line can receive the Guaranteed Income Supplement. You must apply each year and this is not taxable. Spousal Allowance can be paid to qualifying couples receiving only one OAS pension cheque or to widows aged 60 - 65 (Widowed Spouse Allowance until eligible for OAS).

Seniors receiving OAS pension need not spend time in Canada to collect. However, this ruling only applies to Old Age Security and not to other supplementary pensions. Those receiving extra pensions such as Guaranteed Income Supplement and Spousal Allowance subsidies are only collectable for six months from the day you leave Canada.

Canada Pension Plan (CPP) and Quebec Pension Plan (QPP) are financed through payroll deductions and have been since 1966. If you retire at age 60, you can qualify for a reduced amount of this pension or the full amount on retirement at age 65.

CPP can be divided by a 50/50 split between eligible spouses (60 years or older). Those who have lost a spouse are entitled to Canada Pension Plan Survivor's Benefit to age 65.

Contact your local CPP office for more information. And, while you're at it, contact Revenue Canada to see if you can claim your Snowbird medical insurance policy payments as a tax deduction.

More For The Money

While John and I were working, our two substantial and steady salaries allowed us to buy what we wanted. However, living on pensioned income, things changed. Yes, our expenses are lower but, so is the money restocking our bank account each month.

During our first year of extensive travel we spent whatever we wished on "toys" for ourselves plus many gift and souvenirs for everyone back home.

Our style of living changed the second year because, the reality was, if we wanted to continue exploring this way, we had to find ways to make every dollar count. The following dollar stretchers helped us to cut daily living expenses and some of these may be helpful to you.

- When we visit a place, we like to savour the flavour of the area by relishing the different cuisine from local restaurants. A lot of these places include early dinner specials and buffets, so dining out gives us a treat without breaking our budget. Having lunch at an expensive restaurant is more affordable than dinner. Lunch time meals are also more casual so the relaxed dress of most RVers is perfectly acceptable.

- When it is practical, visit popular "hot spots" during the off or fringe seasons. The restaurants, campgrounds and attractions offer discounts up to 50 percent simply because it's a slow time of year.

  > For example, Florida's warm and sunny climate is beautiful in November or in April. These two off-season months are a perfect time to visit most winter utopias without crowds of tourists.

- If you can't save dollars, collect your nickels or quarters. Empty your pockets and purse of your loose change every night and treat yourself to a special meal or unique gift with your savings.

- In this wash-and-wear age, there really is no need to buy "dry clean only" clothes. Read the labels carefully because some blends, especially cotton and rayon, usually need professional care. On the other hand, many silks and woollens are now washable.

- Look for complex shopping malls with a wide range of bargain merchandise. These shopping meccas may simply be discount stores in a mall, factory outlet stores, or pottery factories (popular throughout the U.S.).

"Yup... it's special RV gas!
Sure it's safe and cheap too."

Note: Williamsburg, Virginia, the home of the "queen" of pottery factories is an immense shopping facility. An endless variety of merchandise and a vast amount of stock is available at extremely low prices. This particular (135-acre) complex resembles a giant flea market - only here all merchandise is new. You can find everything from silk flowers and craft supplies to Christmas decorations, kitchen stuff and linens. Fabric, household accessories, hardware, plants, plus so much more, highlight the inventory and every item is reasonably priced. It's a fun and interesting place to visit.

- Outlet malls are the latest form of discount shopping. Manufacturers use this marketing method to off-load first quality products of last year's designs, overruns, over-stocked merchandise, samples, seconds, irregulars and discounted articles - all at very low prices.

However, shop around and become aware of regular prices of the items you plan to buy at outlet malls. Although many name-brands do sell below retail price, all outlet mall merchandise is not a bargain.

These discount havens are usually located near major highways and, sometimes, the only form of advertising is an extra-large billboard indicating which exit to take to reach the store.

In the U.S., RV discount stores, such as Camping World, stock an extensive line of RV accessories at attractive low prices. Located throughout the U.S., the Camping World chain performs general repair service and RV warranty service plus provides installation of all items sold at the stores. Several Canadian dealers offer competitive prices in their stores as well, shop around at home before heading south for what may not be a bargain.

Use credit cards for convenience but avoid cards that carry an annual fee. Paying the balance in full eliminates costly interest charges. However, be careful when using cards at businesses that charge an extra fee for usage. A prime example of this are gas stations where credit card purchases cost more per gallon than cash purchases. (This practice is very common in the U.S. and there are designated credit card pumps calibrated in a higher dollar amount per gallon. Check the pumps carefully before filling up - even if you're paying in cash and accidentally use the credit card-designated pump, you have to pay that price not the lower cash amount. It's also worth noting that many gas stations in the U.S. require payment before filling up your gas tank.)

Don't assume you must be 65 years old to enjoy senior's bene-fits. Some discounts begin when you reach 50, others start at 55 or 60. In several restaurants if the senior member pays, all members of the party may benefit from the senior's discount. Ask, ask, ask - you'll never know who offers discounts to seniors unless you ask.

Enjoy inexpensive sightseeing tours and look for self-explana-tory tapes to play on your vehicle's cassette player. This is a very comfortable and informative way to explore an area at your own pace and in your own vehicle. These cassettes are available for rent in many tourist areas and they may even be free with your camping fees.

Note: The most interesting pre-recorded auto-tapes that

we've used were on an excursion from Banff to Jasper in Alberta and one that related the history and sites of Louisiana's Cajun country.

In both Canada and the U.S., several welcome centres and tourist bureaus offer coupon books to travellers. At each information office ask the staff if they have any coupon promotions and you could receive some valuable savings.

From Monday to Thursday, provincial and state parks may also offer discounts to senior campers. At several places this discounted price bonus continues on weekends, especially during the off-season. At times, provincial and state parks charge lower camping rates than do private parks. However, in most of these beautiful places visitors must pay an extra day-use fee in addition to the camping fee.

Special Note: Several states don't allow pets into the state parks. Tourist bureaus and camping directories list "no pet" areas. Many campgrounds offer a free day's stay if you camp for a week - you pay for six nights and the seventh one is free. The monthly rate is usually 30 to 40 percent lower than a daily fee.

Wayfarer Explorer RV Club member parks, Good Sam RV parks and KOA (Kampgrounds of America) kamps offer a discount to card-carrying members.

In most areas, reservations during off-season are unnecessary, however, this is not the case for peak travel periods - January to March - in all sun country states.

I'm aware that quite a few RVers like the freedom to roam and travel without reservations. However, unless you want to be turned away from many parks or spend time boondocking in fields behind park walls, making a reservation guarantees you a site at this busy time of year. Vacations will be much more enjoyable if you don't waste time looking for a campsite.

These are only a few of the many ways we extend our pension cheques. To find your special dollar stretchers, talk to other RVers you meet. Most of us love to share our secrets and find out all about yours.

Bookkeeping

Keeping a record of all your expenditures is extremely important for both short vacations and for extensive explorations. Whether you simply make notes in a small booklet for each day or week on the road or you keep records much as I did during our early years of RVing, it is very important to know what you're spending your money on and how much you will need for a later excursion. It doesn't matter whether your destinations are next door or someplace far away, good records make follow-up trip planning a lot easier.

Although my earlier records were kept by entries hand-written into a ledger, all my recorded information is now on the computer and it's easier these days to know our financial status at any given time. If you don't have a computer purchase a ledger with expense columns to keep track of weekly or monthly budgets, maintenance for tow vehicles and RVs, fixed expenses (include due dates) plus gas and unexpected costs. Add any other information pertinent to your lifestyle. Don't forget to include dollar exchange rates.

RVers receiving fixed incomes find it a challenge to cope with rising costs. Good record keeping helps to stretch your money to the maximum. Be thorough, but keep your records as simple as possible. After all, your main objective is to enjoy your travels not be bogged down with enough work to challenge an accountant. ■

Living Comfortably in an RV

After living in a spacious house or apartment, many people wonder about coping in a confined area of an RV. Don't worry, if you travel extensively or live fulltime in your unit, you will soon discover that adapting to a smaller space isn't really a big problem.

While we were working, John and I moved from a four bedroom house to our 32-foot motorhome. The transition was horrendous because, for three months, we had military uniforms, job-related articles, clock alarms and so many extras packed into our motorhome. Although these were important items for our military life, we didn't need them for our road life and it was a big relief to finally off-load those extras.

When our alarm clocks went into storage, our tension went with them. Yes, as fulltimers we do continue to get up early to attend certain events but, now, our internal clock kicks in. Other items that we discovered we could live without were my makeup mirror, John's eight pairs of dress pants, two suits and accessories plus my evening clothes. Although we still dress up for special functions, it's no problem to wear the same outfit two times in row. As we move to different locations we meet new friends who have never before seen our wardrobe.

The easiest way to become comfortable in your RV is to eliminate excesses. After 11 years of a life of travel we find most houses have an excess of wasted space. In a house, instead of having to eliminate things, it's easier to hide them in the back of a closet or crawl space. After all, who knows when you might need that treasure again. In our garage sale extravaganza we sold $1,700 of valuable junk that we spent 25 years collecting.

Most RVers are experts at extending space and each one of us is only too happy to share these travel tips with anyone who will listen. The following are some other ways to ease your transition from a house to your home-on-wheels.

- At RV shows listen to as many product demonstrations as time allows. It's to your benefit to learn every detailed fact about RVs - both inside and out.
- Study the information with the same intensity as you would a promotional course at your work place. Ask dealers and the people conducting seminars what everything does and how it works.
- Include questions on such things as weight limits, RV appliances and operation of the levelling devices.
- Add personal touches to your unit.

Luxuries and extras make your RV a special place. If your house had lace and frills, carry that decor into your RV. For instance, I have silk flowers displayed everywhere, silver candle holders on my dinette table and silver wine goblets in the cupboard. These travel well in our motorhome and they were very much a part of our life in our house. Do whatever is necessary to be comfortable and cosy, albeit on a smaller scale.

Although an RV is compact, it's not necessary to live without the comforts of home. Carrying favourite "toys" and appliances on board enhances RV travel, just find easy-to-reach places to stow them. When you must dig for something, it doesn't take long to discover it's easy to live without it.

RVers who join RV club chapters and attend rallies benefit ten-fold from the fellowship and knowledge of the other attendees. Friendships emerge as RVers take part in area tours, potlucks, catered meals, campfires and entertainment. Besides keeping busy, everyone has a good time.

At large rallies, activities include seminars covering all facets of RVing. You can learn so much about the RV lifestyle and your RV from these informative sessions. Speakers discuss engine performance plus talk about and demonstrate accessories such as propane appliances, your 12-volt battery system or converters and inverters. The more you learn, the more you're able to share with others - and, the more you will enjoy RVing.

Read and understand all literature received with your unit. Understanding RV warranties reduces any problems you may experience during a breakdown. Stressful situations are easier to handle when problems don't become overwhelming. Knowing exactly what insurance you have or what each warranty covers prevents disasters when trying to obtain reimbursements later.

New RVers should travel and live in their RV as much as possible - look for campgrounds close to home. Getting use to the idiosyncrasies of your unit can be enlightening as well as a learning experience. The year before John and I retired we spent most of the summer living in our motorhome. What an education that was!

I mention this next point quite frequently but, it's extremely wise for both pilot and co-pilot to be comfortable driving the unit. On our trip south this year, we met a couple in Amarillo, Texas, who, due to a non-life threatening medical problem, had to frequently change drivers. Up to that point, the husband had done most of the driving but had developed problems with his legs which prevented him from sitting in one position for extended periods. Since both were adept at handling their motorhome, they simply traded places every few hours and continued their journey. The trip would have ended abruptly if Mary hadn't felt comfortable driving their coach. Excellent places to practise are shopping centre parking lots - after hours and on holidays, of course.

One thing is certain, when life in your RV becomes commonplace you will never miss the spacious comforts of your other house. In the beginning, when we parked in the driveway of friends or relatives, they frequently asked us to come inside to sleep in a "real bed." Our reply - "We have a real bed, a real shower, a real bath and a real home." Over the years, although some people still can't understand our lifestyle, most no longer ask us to leave our RV home.

Our visits are more enjoyable when we live in our comfortable home-on-wheels in our hosts' driveway and simply spend time socializing in their spacious houses. Before long you, too, can be extremely content living in an RV and maybe even wonder why anyone really needs two homes. This just may be the time to join the many thousands of us who call ourselves fulltimers. ■

The House Dilemma

Now that you have your RV, travelling on a whim is fun. The thought of becoming a fulltimer appeals to your sense of freedom but you do question if it is wise to sell your house or rent it out - just in case. That decision is yours alone and, whatever you decide, neither choice is hassle free and each one carries painful decisions.

To discover the option most suited to both you and your family try to consider realistic economic factors - don't let emotional memories of happy times cloud your decision.

Remember, when a natural disaster such as a flood, fire or tornado destroys a home, finding everyone safe and sound is all that is important. As a result, to objectively dispose of personal acquisitions, think of your home, car, furniture and "can't live without" treasures as inanimate objects.

The following is a list of the pros and cons of renting versus selling.

Renting

❖ **Advantages** - Renting your home keeps your original investment intact and the extra monthly income helps, too. Rent payments should be sufficient to cover mortgage payments (if applicable), property taxes, maintenance, management fees plus any repairs caused by tenants. Of course, it would be ideal if you had some of the rent money left over. Treat rental property as a business. It provides a beneficial tax break. Yes, you must declare the rent received as income but, as long as the house remains a rental property, all expenses become tax write-offs.

❖ **Disadvantages** - Absentee landlords need someone to assume responsibility on their behalf and relying on a friend or relative to keep an eye on your investment may not be the smartest move. Managing a rental property for someone else is a big responsibility.

Since this is a business hire a professional broker to handle the job. Unless you have excellent tenants, costly management fees may dig deep into any rental income you plan to receive.

For instance, if your tenants vacate early or get behind in rent, finding new occupants or dealing with the eviction process costs money. It may even require your personal input or participation. Usually repairs or redecorating are also necessary before new tenants move in.

When John and I faced the sell or rent dilemma it was a surprise to learn that, even if professionals did manage our house as a rental property, we must be part of all decisions, including evictions and screening new tenants. Although every tenant won't cause trouble, one bad experience can easily tarnish your dream.

No one likes to think that situations such as these occur, let alone coping with them from a distance. Problems are aggravating, a nuisance and a huge irritation - especially if all you want is to enjoy your new-found freedom of the RV lifestyle. During our early travels, maintaining an accurate balance in our cheque book was difficult. If we'd chosen to become absentee landlords, the thought of dealing with potential problems from distance places would have been horrendous.

Selling

❖ **Advantages** - The most important point in your decision is the market value of your house. Generally speaking, real estate will always be a profitable investment and you should end up with a large chunk of disposable income.

❖ **Disadvantages** - The decision to sell may not be easy, especially when you've lived in your home a long time. Before deciding, learn the current selling price of houses in your area. Ask yourself if real estate property on a rise or in a decline.

Most RVers realize that wisely invested resale dollars can supplement monthly pension income. Investments providing extra dollars at regular intervals are a sure way to add to your travel pleasures - without the problems or concerns of long-distance property ownership.

When the most beneficial route to follow is uncertain, consider retaining the services of a financial advisor or a broker of any large insurance company. These professionals don't charge fees to advise you about investment options, instead they receive payment from the companies where they place your money.

No One's Home

❖ **Advantages** - This is another choice - just simply lock the doors and go. This way you do not gain monthly equity, however, you also do not pay for any damage caused by unruly tenants.

❖ **Disadvantages** - Even though you're away, you must pay for utilities, snow removal, mail-forwarding and much more. Ensuring an empty house appears lived in takes creativity. If a house looks unoccupied, it sends out an open invitation and a challenge for vandals to gain access. During your absence, routine security checks on your residence is a must. Asking someone to keep on top of what is happening is not only an insurance requirement, it adds tremendous peace of mind while you're exploring North America.

On the other hand, if your empty home is an apartment situated above the second floor or possibly a park model in a secure campground, you could lock the door and walk away after a few minor preparations. Maybe this is the time to downsize your home - keep your treasures but move to a smaller place.

Decisions, decisions, decisions - each situation is unique and individual, only you can make a personalized choice. It's not easy to decide what to do, however, try to remain focused on your new lifestyle. Most definitely, eliminate emotional ties from your final conclusion. Maybe your dilemma will be solved by the answer to this very pertinent question, "Do I need the equity from the sale of my home to finance my RV purchase?" When John and I retired, the resale market was booming and this positive economic fact influenced our decision to let the house go. Ultimately, it was a wise decision.

Another point to consider before making up your mind to sell or rent. Selling our house while still living in it ensured that our home entered the market in show condition. This might not have been the case if tenants had occupied our home for a period of time. We received a good price and, although the market continued to increase after we sold, a wise long-term investment made up for any loss. Even now, we are still happy with our decision and have never looked back. ∎

Should it Stay or Should it Go?

"Pumpkin... do you think that you could let a few of your treasures go?"

Now that you've bought your RV and have decided what to do about your house, the next big question is what to do with important stuff that you've accumulated over the years.

The answer to that question depends whether you plan to simply downsize your residence to allow time for extensive travels or whether you've decided to take the bull by the horns and head out fulltime. In either case, there's no painless way to accomplish the overwhelming task of weeding out your prize possessions. And then there's the daunting task of deciding what to do with your furniture.

First, accept the fact that all furniture and treasures are actually inanimate objects. Whether you decide to keep your collectibles in a storage facility, sell them at a garage sale or give them to the kids, don't despair - you won't eliminate your memories because the memories will stay with you forever.

With these thoughts in mind, the disposal of acquisitions accumulated over the years becomes easier. I realize no major decision is simple, however, when parting with the furniture and accessories that complemented your home, not all choices must be disastrous or heart-wrenching.

If moving into a smaller retirement home, a condo or an RV park model in a campground, simply take valuables to your new home. The collectibles and souvenirs stored at the back of the crawl space in the basement make interesting garage sale items. That is, if the kids or your favourite charity can't use them. Remember, your junk may be somebody else's treasure.

When dismantling a lifetime of memories, many RVers with families ask their kids to choose their favourite things. This way your special mementoes remain family keepsakes. The kids care for them and you can enjoy them as you explain related history during your visits.

In preparation for our new and exciting retirement lifestyle, John and I held a two-day garage sale extravaganza in our drive-way when we sold our house. This enjoyable occasion never seemed to end. Since many mementoes were from my single days, it was fun to watch others appreciate and purchase the treasures I had found irresistible years earlier.

We have no children and were only married four years when we both retired. Shortly into our marriage, new furniture graced our home. On retirement, everything was too new to let is go as used and selling our wedding gifts and valuable keepsakes didn't appeal to us either. We weren't ready to part with new acquisitions such as sheets, blankets, dishes and crystal. There was always the chance that fulltime living in our motorhome wouldn't appeal to us in a few years down the road. So, for the time being, all cherished items went into storage.

We packed keepsakes in well-labelled boxes and found new homes for everything else. Even with all of our planning, John and I made one huge mistake. During the first two years we placed our belongings in an inaccessible long-term storage facility. The main problem with this enclosure is that we had no access to add or subtract anything. When we moved the contents a second time into a self-storage unit, several items from the long-term facility had simply vanished. Yes, they were insured but now we no longer owned those particular household valuables.

We eventually changed to a storage unit where only John and I had a key. This allowed us easy access to dishes, bedding, clothing and other necessities. Simply for the sake of change, it was fun to add new items (from our household cache) to our coach each summer.

This move into a "U-lock-it" facility provided us with one more benefit - with easy access we no longer travelled in an overloaded state. We now store or dispose of every item on board our coach we haven't used during the past year. If I have a favourite special something in the coach then I'd better find a use for it by springtime or it goes.

> When preparing for RV living, it may not be a wise decision to burn all of your bridges during your first years. Be sure, however, to dismantle the costly ones.

Originally our plans included spending a few years of life on the road before settling into one place. We stored sufficient furniture to ensure any future two bedroom apartment would be comfortable. A wise thought at the time, although in retrospect - for us - it was a bad move.

Our first self-storage compartment was large and spacious, however, paying the increasing monthly costs soon became an excessive and unnecessary expense. These costs equalled an amount similar to condominium fees on a small apartment outside of a high-cost-of-living area.

Those wanting to experience fulltime travel in their RV may decide that storing valuables for a few years is the answer. You should, though, liquidate large furniture pieces. When wood and fabric is piled high and sits unused and uncared for over several years, it depreciates very quickly. In time, long-term storage is actually destructive.

Our advice - don't hang on to your furniture. Sell it and replace it as required. Liquidating bedroom, dining room and living room suites displayed in their proper household settings is easier than selling the same items from a storage unit several years later. Trust me, we've tried it!

John and I thoroughly enjoy our travelling lifestyle but, unfortunately, the longer our explorations continued, the more our furniture suffered. Although used furniture is popular, as a resale item it's always an extremely poor investment. Whether you sell in a consignment shop, flea market, newspaper advertisement or at an auction, most owners feel that, even if the pieces are in excellent condition, they just about give away their precious pre-owned home furnishings.

Several years ago we eliminated a few large pieces of our furniture in an auction sale. I can't say that we actually sold it because the price we received was equal to accepting a small fee from someone who paid us so they could take it away. (Don't forget, not only must you consider the original price, you also have to calculate the amount that you've paid for moving your furniture and storage fees over the years. Very rarely will you recoup even a portion of your costs.)

The auction did, however, scale down our possessions so we could fit everything (stacked up high) into a smaller and less costly storage unit. Even with fewer possessions our storage irritations didn't end. Heavy snow during the 93/94 winter damaged the roof of our storage unit. That year, due to the horrendous winter and construction of the storage complex, we had to move our contents five times.

Each move added more stress to our furniture and it was time to let everything go. John and I have no plans to settle anywhere for the foreseeable future and, when we do decide to stop travelling, we'll replace stuff as needed. Unless, of course, our next home is a fully furnished RV park model.

Against our better judgement, we decided to sell the balance of our beautiful furniture at another auction. (It really was our only choice.) We knew that our expensive and quality furniture was becoming slightly tired-looking from long-term storage. However, once again, the low and inappropriate price we received for the three room settings was less than a modest donation to charity. Selling at an auction (with unsealed bids) was and still is a very upsetting experience.

One thing we did learn from this is that buyers take your prized possessions home with them for practically nothing. Forget about receiving a fair market value at any auction - you take what you can get. On the other hand, if we must replace any furnishings in the future, a visit to a small town auction may be our most economical shopping spot. Something good did come out of this. We no longer worry about our furniture wasting away in storage.

Everyone's situation is different. A close friend included their house furniture and contents in the price of their home. Two years later they had no regrets with their decision.

Many fulltimers feel a self-storage facility is the only way to go. Other travellers use a room in their kids' house instead of a U-lock-it-type unit. This works especially well as they can also use that address for a homeowner's insurance policy. John and I still need an area to keep household items such as clothes, linens and treasures close at hand and some place to store our photos, my wedding dress, diplomas and awards as well as our lead crystal, sterling silver serving pieces and more. Our present small and inexpensive storage unit works well - we have room to move around and we can sort through trunks we packed 11 years ago.

Look carefully at all options. Be aware that nothing in this life stays the same. Ideas on what is important change rapidly as you live or travel on the road. At each stage, simply take one day at a time and deal with difficult decisions as they happen. Rest assured, no problem associated with the "good life" is so overwhelming that it should prevent you from enjoying this interesting RV lifestyle. ■

The Homesick Blues

"Great! Just a small get together over the Holidays."

Deciding that extended RV travel is for you is all well and good but, when it comes down to the crunch, inevitably there's a cry, "But I don't want to leave my family!" The homesick blues have struck even before you've left the driveway.

Most fulltiming RVers and long-term travellers reluctantly leave the grandkids when they retire to "play on the road". But, leaving for your new life doesn't mean that you have to cut all ties with the folks back home. Instead, look for unique ways to stay in contact.

Several RVers we've met plan their winter travel destinations to places suggested by children and grandchildren and all parties make arrangements to meet for their own family holidays. That way everyone enjoys a vacation in the sunny south while spending precious time together. Texas, Arizona, Florida, California and Mexico are popular winter getaways. During Christmas and spring break the southern RV parks change from primarily an adult campground to a family reunion party site.

The American Thanksgiving is in late November and some of our friends also take that time to celebrate an early Christmas. They share gifts with visiting family members, decorate a tree with all the trimmings and indulge in the usual Christmas feast. This allows the kids to spend leisurely time with both sets of families. On Christmas day they're free to visit the "other" set back home.

In Canada, Thanksgiving festivities in October are a perfect time for holiday celebrations before Grandma and Grandpa depart. A trip home during the holiday season is another option. Since supplementary medical coverage is changing, habits of extended travellers are too. Several medical insurance companies now offer an inexpensive annual policy for trips that don't exceed ninety continuous days. This type of insurance provides a perfect excuse to fly home at Christmas and break up the time spent out of the country.

We live in a time of mass mobility and frequently kids move because of careers and other employment opportunities. They (and the grandchildren) may work anywhere from one coast to the other. For these grandparents, RV travel is a life saver. It provides the opportunity to visit the children and their families when en route to other exciting destinations. When there's room to move your RV into their driveway, your visit takes on a new dimension since everyone enjoys their own space and family routines don't change much.

Consequently, RVers who live in their unit during family visits place less strain on the lifestyle of both families and, having your own home to retreat to, also provides time for a little rest to recover from the exuberance of active grandchildren.

Whether fulltiming or simply living a distance away from the grandkids, several RVing grandparents invite one child at a time to travel with them during summer vacation. When only one grandchild is with you the event becomes exciting and you can cater to their every wish with undivided attention.

Although we don't have children, John and I are surrounded by a large family. When we started RVing I had five sisters (two are now deceased), along with brothers-in-law, nine nieces and nephews plus great nieces and nephews scattered from Ontario to Nova Scotia. John's sister and brother-in-law and their children and grandkids live in northwest Chicago. During the summer we spend as much time as possible camped near John's aunt who lives in a senior's complex north of Toronto.

Our flexible RV travel schedule offers us the opportunity to visit with family more frequently now than ever was remotely possible while we were working. Since beginning our RV travels, family visits are leisurely and, because we're not always rushing from here to there, a joy. When we live in our hosts' driveway we are close to the action but not so close that we're intruding into their home routine.

Several years ago we added an exciting twist to our travel adventures. Many family members matched their travel destinations with ours. One year we stopped for a visit with John's sister in Chicago, then travelled to Tennessee for a week's stopover in Nashville. There, my sister and her husband joined us to see the sites of Opryland. We then headed for Pompano Beach, Florida where we met another sister and her husband who wanted to enjoy a little relaxation and a lot of sunshine.

That winter, a third sister travelled with us for two months of RV explorations up the west coast of Mexico, into Arizona and southern California. Along the way, several other impromptu reunions with longtime RVing friends complemented this wonderful season.

Not all years blended so well with travels of our friends and family but, it we hadn't been RVing, that 90/91 season wouldn't be part of our most pleasant memories. As experienced RVers we find it fun to share our adventures and most of us spend more time now with our families than we ever thought possible.

Here are a few hints used by grandparents on the road to ensure that the grandkids don't forget them. Sending small tokens to each child from the area you are visiting lets the kids "see" where you are. You can also give them a map before you leave home and send postcards from each stopping spot.

Gifts don't have to be expensive. For instance, younger children will enjoy hearing their own personalized bed-time story. Every region has some kind of legend so make a recording of a story by either reading it directly from a book you've bought or paraphrase the story in your own words to their level of understanding. Older kids may like to read historical brochures along with a referenced road map marked with your route.

Large-hole plastic craft webbing is a fun medium from which to make a variety of things. With a magic marker, trace comic books patterns on the mesh and send it to the kids along with coloured yarn and a large-eye needle. The kids can sew around the design with the thread to create their own special artwork. In an accompanying letter, give simple instructions for them to follow, including the basic cross-stitch pattern.

This craft can be adapted to younger children by cutting a variety of shapes out of cardboard. Punch holes around the outside edge and enclose colourful shoe laces so they can lace through the holes. As well as learning dexterity and simple sewing stitches, they'll also be learning about the different shapes. A set of punch-out cardboard letters from a stationery store is a great learning tool and punch-out numbers can help with basic math.

Most kids like to put stickers on everything. If the grandkids are young, make them a personalized sticker book. Place a line of sticker on a piece of cardboard, leaving room for a second row for the kids to match. Send the left over stickers with a note accompanying your gift.

Take a photo of an unusual tree or flower you see on your travels and explain in a letter its unique characteristics. If possible, include a dried leaf or a few dried petals to illustrate your description.

Collecting sea shells is fun but they are too heavy to store in an RV. A photo of Grandma and Grandpa on the beach with seashore treasures is a lasting memento. Send the kids samples of the different shells with a short note of where you were when you found them. If they still have show-and-tell in their classrooms, suggest that they take the collection to show their class-mates.

Search the discount bins in Wal-Mart, Zellers or K-Mart for end-of-the-line items such as post-it notes, pencils or colourful pin-on buttons that fit inside of a legal size envelope.

Remember, that if you look for easily mailed items that cost under a few dollars, you can enjoy sending these treasures more frequently. Postage for odd-shaped objects usually costs more than the item.

It really makes no difference what you send home, it's hearing from you that matters. Unusual postcards, short letters, small activity crafts, photos or just a note to say "hi" will ensure that you will always be remembered. They will also take a delightful inter-est in your travels.

To leave your family for an extended journey or as a fulltimer is a big decision only you can make. However, on many occasions, children and grandchildren (not to mention the grandparents themselves) are happier with frequent visits for short periods of time. RVs contribute to this type of togetherness. ∎

"I've decided to let Harold use carrier pigeons to stay in touch with his side of the family."

Message forwarding and cell phones are great for keeping in touch with family and friends but another way is through the mail. Of course, mail is the route that companies use to send us bills. Thanks to the many mail forwarding services, RVers moving from place to place can routinely receive their mail without too much difficulty.

John and I can take advantage of our club's free mail forwarding service. A number of other clubs (including many manufacturer clubs) also offer mail forwarding as part of their benefit packages. Some charge a small fee while others charge your account for only the postage used to send the mail on to your destination. For a fee, Canada Post, as well as several businesses (see advertisements in American RV magazines and newspapers) on both sides of the border also forward mail at regular intervals.

The policies of the majority of these services are similar and, as an example, I'll explain how our service works.

Whenever we move from one campground to another, we let

our club's head office know the address of our new location to receive mail. Anyone who writes (or sends bills) to us must put our name and membership number on the envelope along with our club address. Because our name begins with the letter M, our mail leaves the mail forwarding department every Thursday. We phone a 1-800 number before 5:00 p.m. Eastern Standard time every Wednesday to give them our location in the U.S. for the following Monday.

Redirection can be arranged for either a multiple or one-time mailing or we can request "until further notice". By using this service we know that our mail will reach us every week that we're on the road. If we modify our itinerary and don't connect with our package, it's automatically returned to sender after 15 days. As we move throughout Ontario visiting family each summer, our mail follows us to wherever we are staying. In the winter, whether we're in a park for an extended stay or just a few days, with our mail forwarding service we always receive our mail. To cover postage charges, you can forward a deposit or, do as we prefer, have the monthly postal fee charged to a credit card.

We use FMCA's mail forwarding service (located in Ohio) year-round so that we have a U.S. address - a great convenience, especially when applying for a service that requires an American address. It works well for mail-in rebates on purchases and, American camping club mailings and RV magazines reach us faster. Because we are on the road for an extended period and often take advantage of American promotions, we find that by taking out an American club membership and using the U.S.-based address saves us money. Memberships in some clubs, such as Camping World's President Club, are more expensive for Canadians, mostly because of postage costs to send literature across the border. With an American address, we avoid these extra costs. We didn't use a mail forwarding system during those first years and, due to delays at the post office, we frequently chased our mail.

For instance, we were in Texas for a month and a priority post package and three redirected magazines both left an Ontario post office in the same mailing. The magazines arrived in three days and the priority package took 23 days. This was our most exasperating delay but not the only one that upset us. Another time all that reached us was an empty envelope. The contents "fell" out of the envelope and slowly made their way back to our Canadian address. Obviously someone decided to play football with our mail.

During our early travel days, mail to Mexico didn't always arrive at its destination. We were fortunate that my sister spent many winters with us and she hand-carried all precious mail to us. With a mail forwarding service, our weekly package arrived without delay in only seven to 10 days.

Many RV parks won't accept mail sent to campers and suggest having it sent the nearest post office in care of General Delivery. Any postal facility and many customer service counters in stores or RV park offices can provide the postal or zip code of your next destination. Of course, to keep that information close at hand, you can always purchase the cumbersome postal or zip code directories.

Electronic mail is a product of the computer age. To use this system you need a computer, a modem and a telephone. Those with expertise in this field know what I mean, those who can't figure it out (like me), find another source. ■

Paying the Piper

Bill paying is also becoming easier for those of us who live on the road. The longer you enjoy your extended travels, the less mail you receive. RVers going away for the winter can decrease some of their bills by pre-paying pro-rated amounts on water, electric and telephone statements and using cash when travelling eliminates credit card statements. Stop all newspaper and magazine subscriptions and ask the post office or a relative to eliminate all flyers and other junk mail.

Telebanking (banking by phone) is becoming very popular, especially with RVers away from home. For a small monthly fee we can do everything from transfer funds, obtain balances, establish exchange rates, apply for a loan, pay bills and so much more by calling a toll-free number. To make it even easier, a friendly computer "voice" assists you with helpful prompts. Press zero for operator to talk to a real person.

Most banks will also set up a program to pay your bills each month for a small fee. You set the amount, provide the dates and account numbers and the payment comes out of your account.

Many business, especially insurance companies, offer pre-authorized payment deductions taken directly out of your account. You must send a voided cheque to the company you owe money to. That company, in turn, forwards the information to the bank to be filed and, when the bank receives notification of the bill, payment will automatically be deducted from your account.

Banking Power Of Attorney

To ensure that your bills back home are paid on time when you are on the road, you may consider appointing a banking power of attorney.

For the first six years of our travels, we asked a relative to gather and send us our mail, which worked rather well. Since it is a necessity to have a legal address for vehicle registration, driver's licences, insurances, investments, income tax, voter's list and passports, etc., this same relative allowed us to share his home, address and phone number. At the time, he was also our banking power of attorney and could write cheques, pay bills and deposit money on designated accounts. To keep everything in one neat package, he was also our executor.

My sister is now our banking power of attorney and she has banking access to our accounts. As our banking power of attorney, she opens any "official" mail that arrives at her house addressed to us. She sorts through our mail, writes cheques for all bills then, bundles up all the mail (including copies of bills paid), and forwards everything to our destination campground via our mail-forwarding service.

My sister also deposits any cheques and withdraws cash if we ask her. The only stipulation from the bank on the required banking power of attorney permission letter is that, if we die and she writes any cheques after our death, she is responsible for repaying the money to our estate.

Filing Income Tax

During the early years, our power of attorney prepared our tax returns. He would mail everything to us for signatures and we'd return the forms for final preparation and submission. We then switched to a private service that forwarded us a prepared return which we signed and returned by registered mail for submission. At present, our tax service files our returns by E-mail.

By utilizing all the ways to keep in touch with those "back home", you eliminate a lot of frustration and the energy you save can be channelled to where it properly belongs, finding even more ways to enjoy your travels across the roads of North America. ■

Working on the Road

"Actually retired Air Force old boy, why do you ask?"

As a Canadian, to work in another country you must have a work visa or, in the U.S., a green card. Although these are not impossible to obtain, before you apply for one, there are some ramifications that affect your Canadian status.

For instance, when employed in another country, according to that country, it becomes your place of residence for income tax purposes. Applying for and obtaining work visas may eliminate Canadian benefits such as provincial medical coverage. (There are exceptions to this rule, so check with your provincial Ministry of Health.)

Although many RVers do earn money on the road by becoming creative, holding a job in its true sense is not feasible. The following are some ways RVers add extra money to their budget.

I am one of many who send stories to several magazines about our interesting travels. Some RVers exchange services such as general park maintenance for free camping. They run errands, cut grass, do electrical repairs and keep up with building maintenance. No money changes hands so, technically, you're not employed.

Another friend is a bookkeeper. She works two afternoons a week in exchange for a portion of her campsite rent. Others fill in at the campground gift shop for a similar agreement.

The Work Kamper News and Workers on Wheels are two U.S. publications that list seasonable employment opportunities for RVers. Although, the majority of jobs do not apply to Canadians who don't have a green card, it's worth a one-year subscription to get some idea of what is available.

If you like to bake, take orders for special pies or cakes from fellow campers. Ask if you can sell fresh bread or pastries in the campground store. You might even enquire if it's possible to use the clubhouse kitchen to do your baking during the off-hours.

Occasionally park management likes to have bakers on-site. They may even exchange camping fees for a ready supply of sweets to sell to park residents with morning coffee. The park supplies ingredients, receives the profits and you camp in sun country for "free".One Arizona resort that we stayed in is very busy. Since the park manager doesn't live on-site, the campground owners employ two host couples. Although they alternate weeks, one couple is always on call to answer park phones, respond to after-hours emergencies and to make sure that late arrivals have sites. These people are also paid with rent-free camping sites.

This same park also employs a winter resident to run the kitchen. Several times a week, the resort hosts special meals such as Saturday morning breakfasts, special dinners, snacks for dances and provides donuts and muffins for morning coffee. The kitchen has many volunteers to help in the preparation for these functions but the overall planning and co-ordinating is done by one key person in exchange for campsite rent.

U.S. national and state parks as well as the Bureau of Land Management facilities all employ RVers as on-site hosts. Duties and hours of work are minimal and payment is free camping.

Other tips to earn money include a gift-wrapping service (this is especially lucrative during the Christmas season), washing and waxing vehicles to protect them from the sun's harmful rays and, even yard care at resorts where seasonal renters are responsible to keep things neat and manicured.

Of course, there are always odd jobs such as babysitting, pet sitting and walking or, if you have a computer, preparing letters and documents.

One person we know is very knowledgeable about RV repair. As a favour to park members, he performs repairs on-site. His repair service is a hobby and any payment he receives for his inexpensive charges is "cash only" without receipts. This RVer has managed to establish a prosperous non-business which adds considerably to his travelling fund.

We've met RVers who perfected the art of window tinting, upholstering and carpet laying. These crafts provide additional income during their travels. Doing favours by adding extras and updating unit interiors for RVers in some parks is one more way to supplement travel expenses.

Another Canadian friend does the chores that others may hate. For instance, he earns pocket money by washing RVs and awnings. Other RVers use their cars to deliver the 5:00 a.m. papers to subscribers throughout the resorts.

One RVing friend is a retired dressmaker who utilizes her skill to create designer jackets. Making and selling her creations keeps her busy and supplements her living budget.

My sewing machine also receives a good work-out during our travels. I design my special line of hand-painted sun clothes plus reproduce unusual crafts. Frequently, I make these items for personal use and they also serve as fun gifts for family and friends. If I have any extras, I sell them when we return to Canada.

Numerous campers at RV resorts in the sunny south create exquisite crafts to sell from rented tables at area flea markets and craft shows. Most full-service parks hold monthly craft sale days for both local residents and visitors.

Many RVers make jewellery from the beautiful shells, stones

and semi-precious gems they collect along the way. Not only do they sell well at resort craft sales, quite often they are in demand at campgrounds in Canada.

If you are planning to stay in an area for an extended time or, return to the same area each year, you may want to consider arranging to sell your creations at a local shop on consignment. Although no one we've met has become wealthy by selling crafts, making the items is a satisfying and enjoyable way to fill the quiet hours.

It's difficult for RVers to find time to do everything they would like to do. Many mornings I begin writing at 5:00 a.m. because this time frame doesn't interfere with our busy retirement schedule. Some hobbies and tasks are extremely time-consuming but, even the small amount of cash you receive could make the difference between exploring North America or filling each day up with a dead-end job. Although, in most cases, working on the road tops up a travelling budget, it's difficult to earn a sufficient amount to live on.

Work as you previously knew it may not be possible while travelling. However, some enjoyable activities can add small amounts of cash to the budget and give you "free" camping with full hookups.

Residency Changes

Legally no one can visit any country for longer than six months without special visas. From a tax point of view, visitors who remain longer than six months in another country (U.S., Mexico, etc.) are considered residents and should pay taxes. The host country wants tax money from every inhabitant.

Canada's economy is similar to the U.S. As a result it's not easy for a Canadian to immigrate but it's not impossible either. Before you decide to make a change in your country of residence, check into all facts such as medical costs, residency requirements and tax rules - some states tax pension money as well as long-term investment benefits over and above the U.S.

federal government.

Moving south may seem to be perfect for you and your family, however, you may discover that the initial incentives lose some of their lustre. Contact lawyers, embassies or consulates on both sides of the border to obtain the most up-to-date information available. ■

Enjoying the Good Life

"We've never been to any of these places. Harold just likes to look well travelled!"

Our family and friends who haven't had the opportunity to enjoy the RV lifestyle are always asking us if we get bored. Bored! I just wish that we had the time to fit our busy schedules into a 24-hour day.

We spend most of our time moving around and exploring new and exciting destinations. We've enjoyed the sights of RVing hot spots - Arizona, Mexico, Florida and Texas - as well as our own vast and beautiful country. In the winter, you'll usually find us camped at some southern oasis in one of the many parks dedicated to the RV lifestyle.

Although some of these parks only have basic facilities, others are five-star resorts overflowing with amenities such as weight rooms, billiard tables, pools, hot tubs, saunas, clubhouses, sport facilities and fully-equipped wood-working rooms. To avoid the winter rush to sun country, we simply find a park that we think will suit us from a campground directory and book early for a three month reservation. Booking for an extended stay is usually cheaper.

Once we arrive at the park, we set up house, install a phone and cable TV, arrange for newspaper delivery and become pampered park residents. It's like a holiday for us where we can relax and stretch out.

Most parks have newsletters to let campers know what events are taking place in the park and surrounding area. Popular activities such as golf, shuffleboard, aerobics, aquafit, dance lessons and card games intermingle with craft and ceramic classes, instructions in water and oil painting plus a whole host of special theme nights. This is our usual choice of a winter getaway but, last year, we and many of our RV friends changed destinations every one or two weeks.

Some evenings, groups get together for impromptu music fests or a tail-gate pizza party. As well, most parks plan activities such as dances, pot-luck and special dinners.

I could go on and on about the extensive array of park activities. Each resort differs from the next but, in most cases, it's absolutely impossible to participate in everything. We've found that when RVers first retire or, are on their first extended vacation, they take to the road they try to see everything at once. It's difficult to accept the idea that returning to work in two weeks is a thing of the past. Most of us "run" during our first getaways. Eventually, everyone slows down but, 11 years later, we still find the lack of time to do everything our biggest problem.

There are so many things RVers like to do in retirement, from reading a book there was never time for in the "old" life to enjoying leisure hours by the pool, taking long hikes, biking or walking throughout the park. Just plain socializing with others not confined to a schedule is another benefit of RV living. And, it's certainly not boring.

RVers moving from park to park can enjoy long forgotten hobbies or take the time to learn a special craft. Each area they visit caters to different interests so, whatever your interest, there will be something perfect for you.

The most common complaint we hear from full and part-time

retirees is, "I don't know how I ever found the time to work eight hours every day." Life is so full when everything you do is enjoyable.

Keeping busy doing what you wish to do is why RVing seniors remain so young. There are people in their 80s still moving around calling all of North America their home. And, by that time, many RVers trade their home-on-wheels for a park model, they still continue to enjoy resort festivities - without travelling to new horizons.

During our years in the military, every job had a description. I like to think the following applies to most RVers.

What is an RVer?

❖ Skills

- Must have the ability to trip plan exciting and scenic routes between destinations.
- Stretch a week's allowance to include attractions en route but never go over budget.
- The ability to be a friend and goodwill ambassador representing your country and the RV world.

❖ Duties

- Take part in every interesting event your present resort offers. Join RV clubs/chapters and participate in events.
- With the balance of each day, you will explore the surrounding area as well as trying to discover and visit all available bargain or shopping areas. Be extra careful not to miss important sights along the way.

❖ Benefits Package

- In the evening, you have earned the time to relax and enjoy a little TV, visit friends, play cards or read. You can also indulge in toe-tappin' music or any other miscellaneous activity that strikes your fancy.
- If the RVing lifestyle appeals to you, don't wait to follow your dreams. RVers we meet who now spend many months on the road can't understand why it took them so long to begin their

adventure.

- When John and I began RVing, no one was greener or as inexperienced as we were. We found a campground 20 minutes from work and spent as much time as possible in our motorhome.

Fortunately, for us, our neighbours, Jack and Eunice McCleary from Florida, were seasoned RVers. They took us under their wing while they explained, coddled, protected and educated us on many facets of RVing. They also shared their hints and secrets to successful living and travelling in an RV. Their hospitality set a precedent for us to do the same for inexperienced RVers we meet on our travels.

Over the years John and I have spent so much time explaining the basics to new RVers and, as our first year rolled into many, we decided that the simplest way for us to reach the maximum amount of people was to include everything in a guidebook.

Completing Spirit of the Open Road was a long haul over a very rocky road but, nevertheless, I count it as one of my finest accomplishments - other than marrying my best friend, John, four years before we retired.

Without the help, encouragement and the never-ending patience of John and other staunch supporters, this dream may never have become a reality.

I hope this book answers most of the questions that you may have or, at least explains how to obtain information when required. For your convenience I've included a directory of addresses and, were possible, provided telephone numbers so that you can continually update your information.

When seeking information, call an office several times to talk to different officials (especially from a government office). Do this anonymously, if you wish, and if you get (like I do) a variety of explanations for the same question, ask why. Assess the information and decide how each situation applies to you.

With a little planning and preparation for the unexpected,

you'll prevent upsetting surprises. Preparation is the first step to exciting RV travels. And, if you travel informed, emergencies and problems become less traumatic.

John and I proudly display our motto "Goodbye Tension: Hello Pension" on the front and back of our coach and car. Registered in Ontario, our motorhome licence spells out R DREEM and our car reads R GO 4 and, on the road, we tune in to Channel 14 on the CB. When our paths cross, honk your horn and give a wave to say "Hi!"

During our travels last fall we saw a sign on a billboard outside a small Ontario town. Though I can't remember the name of the town, the words on the sign stuck in my mind. They were a perfect description of the RV lifestyle.

"We meet, we part until we meet again." Happy travelling. ∎

Canadian Customs and Importing

Department of Transportation
1-800-511-7755

Registrar of Imported Vehicles
1-800-333-0558

Revenue Canada/Customs
1-800-461-9999

Canadian RV Associations

Canadian Recreational Vehicle Association (CRVA)
670 Bloor Street West
Suite 200
Toronto, Ontario M6G 1I2
(416) 533-7800

Canadian Standards Association (CSA)
178 Rexdale Blvd.
Rexdale, Ontario M9W 1R3
(416) 747-4000

Recreation Vehicle Dealers Association of Canada (RVDA)
#209 - 20353 - 64th Avenue
Langley, British Columbia V2Y 1N5
(604) 533-4010

Canadian RV Clubs

Federation Quebecoise de Camping et de Caravanning, Inc
4545, avenue Pierre-de-Coubertin
CP1000 succ. M
Montreal, Quebec H1V 3R2
(514) 252-3003

Wayfarer Explorer RV Club
1235 Bay Street
Suite 1000
Toronto, Ontario M5R 3K4
1-800-999-0819
In the Toronto area call: (416) 782-8386

Canadian RV Magazines

Camping Canada Magazine
2585 Skymark Avenue
Unit 306
Mississauga, Ontario L4W 4L5
(905) 624-8218

Gazette (The)
1235 Bay Street
Suite 1000
Toronto, Ontario M5R 3K4
1-800-999-0819
In the Toronto area call: (416) 782-8386

RV Times
Box 160, 129 West 2nd Avenue
Qualicum Beach, British Columbia V9K 1S7
(604) 752-8266

RV Traveller
174 Baseline Road, West
London, Ontario N6J 1V7
1-800-449-4426
In the London area call: (519) 438-8221

Wagon Train Travelers
117 Dumfries Avenue
Brampton, Ontario L6Z 2W6
1-888-762-3278
(905) 846-0151

Canadian Handicap Conversion Companies:

Bahn Corporation
8 Grand Avenue
Kitchener, Ontario N2K 1B3
(519) 744-8754
Fax: (519) 744-6861

Freedom Motors
3190 Ridgeway Drive
Suite 8
Mississauga, Ontario L5L 5S8
(905) 828-1996
Fax: (905) 828-4112

H & H Braund Mfg. Co. (Canada) Ltd.
183 Durham Street, West
Mount Forest, Ontario N0G 2L0
(519) 323-2021
Fax: (519) 323-2890

Lyco Products Ltd.
9087B-198th Street
Suite 210
Langley, BC V1M 3B1
(604) 888-5764
Fax: (604) 888-3952

Membership Camping

Campers Club of America (CCA)
1-800-369-2267

Coast To Coast (CCC)
1-800-368-5721

Resort Parks International (RPI)
1-800-635-8498
(reservations : 1-800-456-7774)

Thousand Trails (TT)
1-800-321-2332

Provincial/Territory Medical Information Office

Alberta - (403) 427-0259

British Columbia - (604) 952-1742

Manitoba - (204) 786-7101 or
for hearing impaired service (204) 774-8618

New Brunswick - (506) 453-2161

Newfoundland - (709) 729-3108

North West Territories - In Canada: 1-800-661-0830;
elsewhere (403) 979-7411

Nova Scotia - (902) 468-9700

Ontario - 1-800-268-1153

Prince Edward Island - (902) 368-5858

Quebec - (418) 646-4636

Saskatchewan - (306) 787-3475

Yukon - (403) 667-5209

U.S. Handicap Conversion Companies:

ADC Services
15 West Fullerton Street
Addison, Illinois 60101
(708) 628-6909
Fax: (708) 628-7008

Accele Electric Inc.
17900 Crusader Avenue
Cerritos, California 90703
(310) 809-5090
Fax: (310) 860-7650

Ahnafield Corp.
3219 West Washington Street
Indianapolis, Indiana 46222
(317) 636-8061
Fax: (317) 636-8098

Camping World
National Supply Company
P.O. Box 90018
650 Three Springs Road
Bowling Green, Kentucky 42102-9018
(502) 781-2718
Fax: (502) 781-2775

Gresham Driving Aids Inc.
P.O. Box 930334
Wixom, Michigan 48393-0334
(810) 624-1533
Fax: (810) 624-6358
U.S. only 1-800-521-8930

H & H Braund
730 East Michigan Avenue
Battle Creek, Michigan 49016
(616) 965-2371
Fax: (616) 965-2389

MASE International
603 East William Street
Maumee, Ohio 43537-3401
1-800-727-6273
Fax: 1-800-827-6273

Mobility Products Corporation
6270 Brookhill Drive
Houston, Texas 77087
1-800-972-5438
Fax: (713) 645-2714

U.S. RV Clubs

Camper Clubs of America
2338 S McClintock Drive
Tempe, Arizona 85282
(602) 966-3085

Camping World
P.O. Box 90017
Bowling Green, Kentucky 42102-9017
1-800-626-9017

Escapees (SKP'S)
100 Rainbow Drive
Livingston, Texas 77351
1-800-976-8377

Family Campers and RVers (FCRV)
4808 Transit Road, Building 2
Depew, New York 14043-4704
1-800-245-9755

Family Travel Trailer Association (FTTA)
P.O. Box 5867
Titusville, Florida 32783
1-800-603-1101

Lazy Daze Caravan Club
4303 E Mission Blvd
Pomona, California 91766
(714) 627-1219

Good Sam Club
P.O. Box 501
Agoura, California 91376-9935
1-800-234-3450

Family Motor Coach Association (FMCA)
Membership Chairman
8291 Clough Pike
Cincinnati, Ohio 45244-2796
1-800-543-3622

You've read the book...

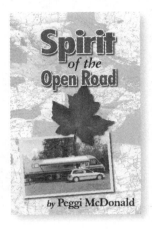

...now enjoy the lifestyle!

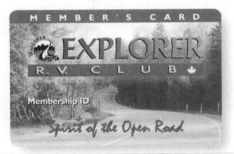

Call: 1-800-999-0819

for information about the Explorer RV Club

Be sure to check out Peggi and John's Website

www.rvliving.net